EVERYTHING FOR

KIDS'
ROOMS

Editor and text
PATRICIA BUENO

Design and typesetting
CARLOS GAMBOA PERMANYER

Production
JUANJO RODRÍGUEZ NOVEL

Translation
MARK HOLLOWAY

Copyright © 2004 Atrium Group

First published by: Atrium Group de ediciones y publicaciones, S.L.
c/ Ganduxer, 112
08022 BARCELONA

Tel: +34 932 540 099
Fax: +34 932 118 139
e-mail: atrium@atriumgroup.org
www.atriumbooks.com

ISBN: 84-95692-77-5
Dep. Leg.: B-47004-03

Printed in Spain by
Anman Gràfiques del Vallès, S.L.

149, 161
€ 28.00

INDEX

The main ingredient for decorating an infant's room is imagination. Not only is imagination vital when it comes to inventing dream worlds, but essential to being able to make that effort to see through the child's eyes and conceive what we would like to have in our surroundings if we were his or her age.

Evidently, determined tastes and necessities accompany each of the growing stages and, therefore, the surroundings designed for a child should be adaptable to his or her growth and to the endless chain of changes that this implies. In the same way, an infant's room should be able to accommodate everything from the basic pieces of furniture required for a newborn baby to the countless belongings possessed by an adolescent while offering, at each stage, an environment adequate for each age able to stimulate and strengthen the personality of each child.

To help parents with the task of decorating rooms according to age, this book has been divided into three large chapters that correspond to the main stages of growth:

–*From 0 to 2 years: rooms for babies* in which pastel colors, coordinated environments, fabrics with cheerful infantile motifs along with versatile furniture that can be modified so as to grow with the child predominate.

–*From 3 to 11 years: rooms for children* in which the most important thing is to have a large space to play in. The main feature of these spaces is the modular furniture that allows for compositions that maximize the amount of space available and that can be modified according to the necessities of each moment.

–*From 12 to 16 years: rooms for adolescents:* private spaces in which there should be enough space to store belongings, to install a comfortable area for study and, of course, for intimacy.

Each chapter is illustrated with hundreds of proposals from the top designers and manufacturers specialized in the sector which show everything from well-established styles with a certain rustic or classical taste to the latest tendencies which fill the room with daring colors and innovative designs to create contemporary and extremely functional environments.

From these proposals, each one of us should try to find those pieces with are most suitable for the spaces we have available to us and combine them with details that will personalize and make the space unique and as a result create an environment which our children will be able to identify with and feel to be something of their own. To achieve this, it is imperative that parents take the tastes that their children begin to have of their own into consideration as soon as possible so as to start collaboration on the choice of colors and fabrics and, above all, to have fun and imagine new worlds full of quality and fantasy together.

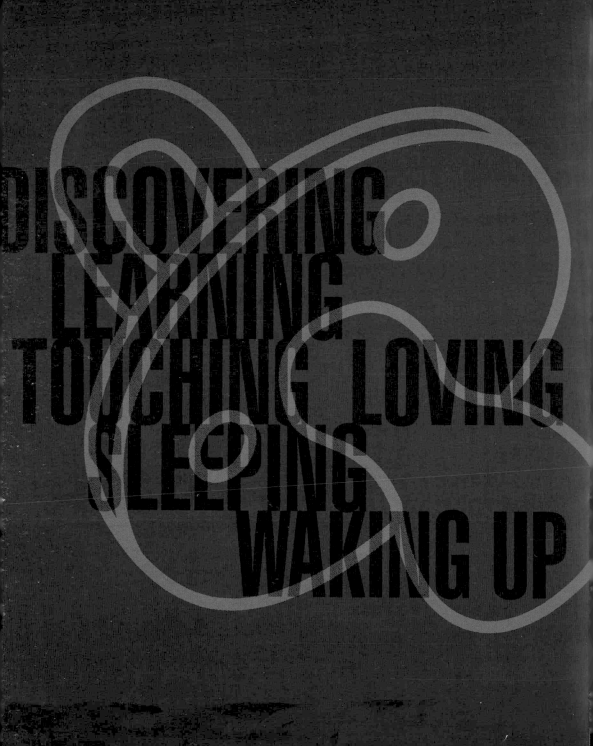

DISCOVERING
LEARNING
TOUCHING LOVING
SLEEPING
WAKING UP

A newborn baby needs very little furniture in its room. In fact, the only really indispensable element is its cot. However, it is evidently very difficult to renounce the temptation of converting the newborn's room into a place full of fantasy and giving free rein to our imagination. Decorating the baby's room gives the parents an opportunity to play with colorful magic worlds that are full of characters from children's tales that come to life in fabrics, furniture and accessories. It is an opportunity to go back to our own infancies through the eyes of our children.

The market offers countless possibilities for furnishing rooms in all styles and for all budgets that not only offer a wide range of solutions as far as aesthetic considerations are concerned, but that considerably augment comfort as much for the children as for the parents.

Over the last few years, the attention and investment dedicated to this area have grown noticeably. This is due to the increase in quality of life and to families becoming more aware of the necessity for children to enjoy beneficial environments that stimulate their incipient senses and favor an adequate development which, at the same time, strengthens their various infantile capacities such as a sense of independence or a consciousness of having one's own space.

As a result, other elements are added to the basic cot among which the bathtub, the chest of drawers, the changing table, the wardrobe, the toy chest or basket along with coordinated color schemes that match everything from the wall paper to the trimmings and cot cover stand out. In general, parents tend to look for a kind of integral decoration in which the elements coordinate among themselves to create a unified environment that transmits harmony, tranquillity and happiness. However, we should bear in mind that children grow very quickly and that it is therefore advisable to avoid using overcharged or highly infantile motifs that rapidly fall out of fashion.

A worthy resource is the use of light colors and simple lines as the unifying factor for the decoration and then the 'magic' touches can be introduced by adding accessories that can easily be replaced as the child grows.

Another option is to buy evolutionary furniture that grows with the child. Although the initial outlay may be greater, in the long term, articles of this nature often tend to work out cheaper given that they are useful for a longer period of time. In this group, cots that become beds, chests of drawers that are changing tables and baths all in one (if they are of a convenient height), bath-changing tables, chairs that grow with the child and, in general, all those pieces of versatile and flexible multi-use furniture such as wardrobes or shelves (these can later cease to exhibit fluffy toys and form part of a study area) are all found.

As far as materials are concerned, wood, especially pine, oak or beech, tends to be the star in this room although there is currently a trend toward furniture lacquered in light colors. It is preferable to opt for natural materials in fabrics such as 100% cotton or linen.

Whatever the case, always make sure that each piece of furniture acquired complies with safety requirements in force and that they have been officially approved. This indicates that the articles have passed technical inspections and quality controls that are necessary to guarantee the baby's complete security. Every product must comply with specific regulations that should appear on the label. To give examples of this, here are some basic rules and regulations: make sure that the distance between the bars of the baby's cot or playpen is no greater than 6 cm and that they are firm and structurally resistant. Use a mattress that fits into the cot perfectly and check that neither the cot nor changing table has any elements that protrude, can be extracted or are sharp and, as a consequence, may cut.

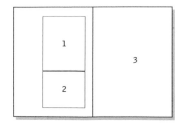

1. Cot "ELEOCO'" from Cyrus Company Bambino■
Manufactured with a metal frame and cushioned interior with washable linen cover■
2. Cot "MANDARINO" from Cyrus Company Bambino■
Manufactured with a metal frame and cushioned interior with washable linen cover■
3. Cot from the collection "BELLAS BALLROOM" design from Amanda Heath for Wigwam Kids■
Artisanal cot handmade in beech painted white. The base can be set at two different heights. Dimensions: 75 cm high × 76 cm wide × 160 cm long (photo: Mark Seager, The Picture House UK)■

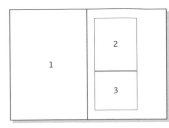

1. Furniture collection "COQUILLAGE BLANC" from Tartine et Chocolat■
The softness of the white and natural tones along with the delicate finishes of the furniture gives this room a certain romantic air■
2. Collection "SOL MAGIC" from Schardt■
The way the fabrics and the pieces of furniture have been combined characterize this group■
3. Furniture collection "PILOT" from Schardt■
Beech with a soft white scaling combined with wickerwork drawers and complemented with fabrics■

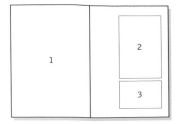

1. Room from the collection "BALU-NI" from Hülsta■
The furniture from this collection grows with the child. The cot, for example, converts into a small bed. The different pieces combine natural beech with surfaces lacquered in pastel colors which offer numerous possibilities■
2. Group of color coordinated fabrics from the collection "AEIOU" from Belino■
Everything has been perfectly coordinated in this room for the baby, from the clothes to the curtains■
3. Furniture collection "VERONA" from Micuna■
All of the furniture in this collection is manufactured in beech. The finishes combine natural wood with white and ivory. The mattress base can be set in three different positions so as to adapt to the baby's age■

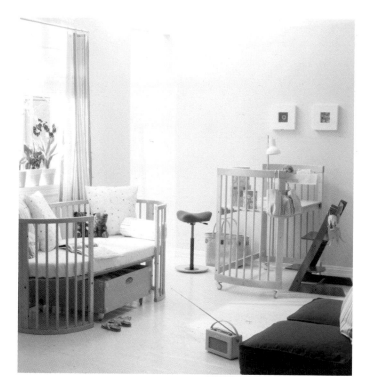

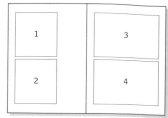

| 1 | | 3 |
| 2 | | 4 |

1. Environment decorated with furniture from the firm Stokke■
Here, above all, the bed for infants "SLEEPI JUNIOR", designed by Grønlund and Knudsen and manufactured in beech, stands out. The side opening allows it to be used as a sofa. The bed is assembled by adding new elements to the cot■
2. Bedside table from the collection of decorative accessories "CONEJITOS POM-POM" from Tirimilitín■
3. Furniture collection "MAR" from Micuna■
All of the elements in this collection are manufactured in natural beech. The base of the bed can be set at three different heights■
4. Furniture collection "DUNA" from Micuna■
Cot and bath-changer manufactured in solid pine. The decorative wall lamps in hand painted resin are optional■

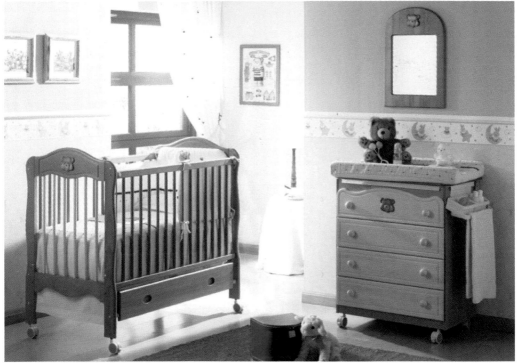

149, 161

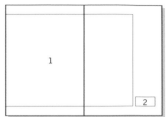

1. Furniture collection "TRANVÍA" from Babymobel∎

All of the furniture is manufactured in pine stained to a fir wood or hazel wood color. Dimensions: chest of drawers, 102 cm high × 100 cm wide × 58 cm long; wardrobe, 188 cm high × 92 cm wide × 53 cm long; the cot is available in two dimensions: 120 × 60 cm and 140 × 70 cm (the larger can be converted into a bed)∎

2. Carpet from the firm Pasito a Pasito∎

This carpet, in the form of a toy bear, is one of the many decorative elements that can introduce an infantile touch to the baby's room∎

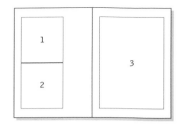

1. Bedclothes set ''LE REINE DES GRENOUILLES'' from Jacadi■
The pieces in this collection are made of 100% cotton with a 100% polyester filling that has received anti-bacterial treatment. In the photo: the cot guard, quilt, pillow and child's sleeping bag. The use of quilts, pillows and eiderdowns are recommended once the baby is 18 months old■

2. Bedclothes set ''LES FÉES'' from Jacadi■
The articles in this collection are made of 80% cotton and 20% polyester anti-bacterial treated fabric. The dimensions of the bed set are 120 cm wide × 180 cm long and those for the cot guard 45 cm wide × 210 cm long■

3. Layette ''PASTEL'' from Belino■
This collection includes numerous articles, from canopies to visiting bags, in soft pastel-toned fabrics which give the room a colorful and relaxing atmosphere■

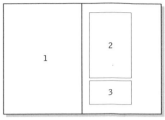

1. Fabrics "Baby Cordelé" from Bolín Bolón▪
The use of 'happy' yellow makes this line stand out. It includes everything from a small cushioned armchair to fabric to make made to measure curtains▪
2. Wardrobe manufactured by Cyrus Company▪
Wardrobe with a door which incorporates an amusing lamp in the form of a bear in natural wood▪
3. Trunks from the collection "Tina & Tin" from Tirimilitín▪
These friendly trunks, in addition to being highly decorative, help to keep the toys in order▪

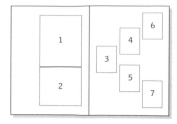

1. Cot from the collection "Trésor" from Jacadi.

Cot with beech frame and base to which canopy and matching mosquito net can be added. A pedal to stop rocking when desired is included. Made to measure covering in white piqué. Dimensions: cot, 76 cm high × 86 cm wide × 90 cm long; canopy, 150 cm high.

2. Cot "Barca" from Jacadi.

Cot with wickerwork body and frame in beech. Includes *chambray* covering, 80% cotton and 20% polyester, in sky blue. Dimensions: 90 cm high × 56 cm wide × 95 cm long.

3. Bed set from the collection "Pipo" and wickerwork cradle from Leipold.

4. Bedclothes from the collection "Vivaldi" and wickerwork character with support from Leipold.

5. Bedclothes from the collection "Amrun" and cradle in wood with folding hood from Leipold.

6. Bedclothes from the collection "Tulip" and wickerwork cradle with fixed hood in the same material. From Leipold.

7. Wickerwork cradle on castors and made to measure fabric interior covering from Leipold.

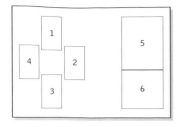

1. Selection of bedclothes and canopy from the collection "LAND-HAUS" and wickerwork cradle. From Leipold■

2. Bedclothes from the collection "CHARLY" and wickerwork cot "AL-ADIN" with optional tray. From Leipold■

3. Bedclothes and canopy from the collection "LEO" and wickerwork cradle with wheels, from Leipold■

4. Fabric collection "MOZART" and wickerwork cradle on castors and optional tray from Leipold■

5. Fabric collection "CORAZÓN DE OSO" from Bolín Bolón■

Complete collection of fabric accessories that stand out for their elegant combination of brown tones and the chain stitch included in many of the pieces■

6. The "CLAIRE" furniture range and combined fabrics from Paidi■

Room in solid pine with a marked rustic air. Dimensions: cot, 89.6 cm high × 76 cm wide × 146 cm long; wardrobe, 194.5 cm high × 95.6 cm wide × 54.5 cm long; chest of drawers (with separate changing table element), 90 cm high × 97.6 cm wide × 55.5 cm long■

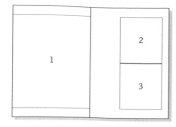

1. Room from the collection "OSLO" from Bébé-Jou■

Group of varnished furniture made in MDF with details such as grooves and leather handgrips that give it a light rustic touch. The bedclothes and canopy are from the "MOOSE" line. Dimensions: cot, 60 cm wide × 120 cm long; chest of drawers, 89 cm high × 109 cm wide × 55 cm long; wardrobe, 178 cm high × 109 cm wide × 55 cm long■

2. Cradle from the collection "CLAIRE" from Paidi■

This rocking wickerwork cradle introduces a note of classical romanticism into the room. Dimensions: 90 cm high × 68 cm wide × 113.5 cm long■

3. Cot with canopy "RÉPLIQUE" from Jacadi■

Frame in solid beech and padded covering in reversible white piqué 100% cotton. Dimensions: 90 cm high (not including canopy) × 50 cm wide × 92 cm long■

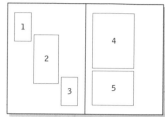

1. Bedclothes from the collection "WENDY" and wickerwork cradle with canopy from Leipold.

2. Bedclothes from the collection "DAMARIS" and cot with metallic canopy and rocking body from Leipold.

3. Fabric collection "WALISA" and cot in wood with turned bars, from Leipold.

4. Bookcase with drawers "ALVEARE" from Cyrus Company.
This original double-sided container element is presented with drawers that are lacquered or stained with water based paints.

5. Cot "GABRIELE" from Cyrus Company.
Wooden cot lacquered or stained with water based paints. The fabric elements can be detached, uncovered and washed.

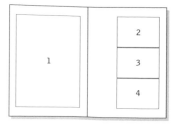

1. Cot from the collection "NUBE" from Babymobel■
Manufactured in MDF lacquered in white and with decorative lamps. A practical optional drawer can be included in the base■

2. The "BRUSELAS" group from Mobilín■
The cot is of a practical convertible design and can be transformed into a small bookcase, a bedside table and a chest. Dimensions: convertible bed, 90 cm high × 80 cm wide and 163 cm long; sifonier, 103 cm high × 90 cm wide × 50 cm long■

3. The "OLAF" range of furniture from Paidi■
The element in natural wood that includes the original bull's eye window is in solid beech. Dimensions: cot, 81.8 cm high × 78.2 cm wide × 148 cm long; chest of drawers (not including the changing table element), 88.4 cm high × 94.7 cm wide × 40.3 cm long; wardrobe, 175.4 cm high × 94.7 cm wide × 56.3 cm long■

4. Room model "MARTA" from Mobilín■
Presented in honey or natural colors. Dimensions: cot, 60 cm wide × 120 cm long; wardrobe, 180 cm high × 117 cm wide × 63 cm long; chest of drawers, 85 cm high × 108 cm wide × 50 cm long■

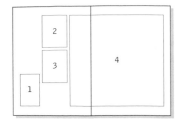

1. Set of bedclothes from the "Tulip" collection and wickerwork canopy from Leipold∎

2. Set of bedclothes from the "Easy" collection and twin wicker-work cots that can be separated. From Leipold∎

3. Convertible cot "Sleepi". Design from Grønlund and Knudsen for Stokke∎

This cot adapts to the growth of the child as it can be converted from a cradle to a bed, sofa, two chairs... It is manufactured in beech in various finishes and colors∎

4. Infant's room "Bombay" from Bébé-Jou∎

The furniture in this collection is manufactured in solid birch combined with elements of woven birch strips. The cot can be converted into a bed. Dimensions: cot, 60 × 120 cm or 70 × 140 cm; wardrobe, 177 cm high × 113 cm wide x 53 cm long; chest of drawers, 89 cm high × 113 cm wide × 53 cm long∎

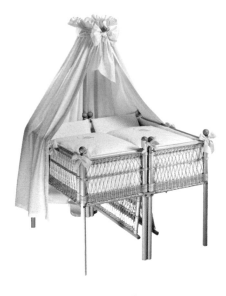

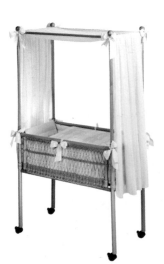

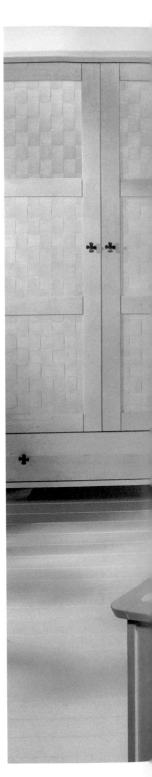

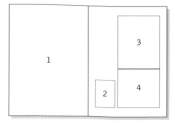

1. Furniture collection "PETITS AMIS SAPIN" from Tartine et Chocolat▪
This group transmits a certain Provençal air as much as in the wardrobe, which imitates forms from antique closets, as in the soft white scaling applied to the furniture▪
2. Changing table "SLEEPI CARE" from Grønlund and Knudsen for Stokke▪
Changing table with adjustable height made in beech and which allows us to have all our accessories at hand. As the baby grows, it can be converted into a desk, a bookcase or, by adding an optional accessory, a practical study table▪
3. The "OSO" layette set from Belino▪
This series of color coordinated fabrics for the baby features a family of bears, one of the traditional motifs preferred by both children and their parents▪
4. Chest of drawers in lacquered wood with forms in relief from the "HIMALAYA" collection from Tartine et Chocolat▪

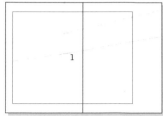

1. Room model "Judith" from Micuna.

Furniture made in beech and painted in semi-mat white with decorative details in sky blue. A drawer can be incorporated in the base of the cot and the chest of drawers also serves as a changing table and bath.

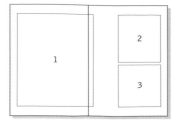

1. The "NOEMÍ" children's furniture range from Babymobel.
Pine furniture with a chestnut stain. The decorative hand-painted ceramic element in the figure of a toy bear is optional. Dimensions of the wardrobe: 185 cm high × 103 cm wide × 57 cm long.

2. Cradle with canopy from Babymobel.
The cradle is manufactured in pine and stained in a dark color. The bedclothes are from the "NOEMÍ" collection.

3. Furniture from the "TENNESSEE" collection from Bébé-Jou.
A group with classical lines manufactured in alno stained in a cherry color. A shelf can be incorporated in the chest of drawers-changing table. Dimensions: cot, 60 x 120 cm or 70 × 140 cm (convertible in bed); wardrobe, 182 cm high × 112 cm wide × 51 cm long; chest of drawers, 89 cm high × 109 cm wide × 55 cm long.

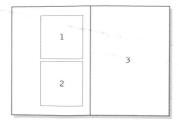

1. Chest of drawers and changing table from the "TRÉSOR" collection from Jacadi.
All of the pieces in this collection are manufactured in pine stained in a honey color and finished in an egg-shell varnish. The drawers in the chest of drawers are set over metal rails with rollers. Dimensions: chest of drawers, 84 cm high × 95 cm wide × 50 cm long; changing table, 9.5 cm high × 56 cm wide × 72 cm long.

2. Cot from the "RÊVE" collection from Jacadi.
Pine frame stained in a honey color and base in sheet MDF that offers three possible positions. Two dimensions: 82 cm high × 68 cm wide × 125 cm long or 82 × 78 × 145 cm.

3. Fabric accessories from the "CA-BALLITO" line from Bolín Bolón.
Amusing collection in soft browns and orange tones that are very comfortable due to the padded material used in many of the pieces.

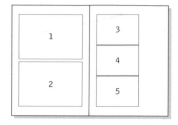

1. Furniture collection "Luna" from Leipold.

A perfectly coordinated range of furniture that combines wood with wickerwork. The cot offers a double base position and can be converted into a small bed. Dimensions: cot, 70 cm wide × 140 cm long; wardrobe, 220 cm high × 158 cm wide × 55 cm long.

2. Furniture collection "Fichte" from Leipold.

The cot allows for two different base positions and converts into a bed. Dimensions: cot, 70 cm wide × 140 cm long; changer with side shelf (optional), 96 cm high × 105 cm wide × 81 cm long.

3. Collection "Grecia" from Mobilín.

This group is finished in a hazel color and includes discrete decorative carvings. Dimensions: cot, 60 cm wide × 120 cm long; chest of drawers (without changer accessory), 82 cm high × 94 cm wide × 49 cm long; wardrobe, 164 cm high × 94 cm wide × 49 cm long.

4. Collection "Fantasía" from Babymobel.

Furniture made in stained pine. The hand-painted decorative element in resin is optional.

5. Group from the "Robin Natural" model from Perelló.

This range stands out for its elaborated details such as the drawer with transparent front. Dimensions: cot (convertible into bed), 60 × 120 cm or 70 × 140 cm; chest of drawers, 94 cm high × 110 cm wide × 55 cm long; wardrobe, 176 cm high × 110 cm wide × 55 cm long; shelf, 27 cm high × 79 cm wide x 19 cm deep.

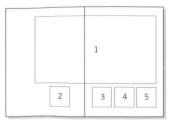

1. Room from the "MARIE" collection from Paidi■
This furniture is available in two different finishes: colored in sycamore or beech. The chest of drawers can incorporate a practical changer accessory. The base can be set in any of four different positions. Dimensions: cot, 85.8 cm high × 86.9 cm wide × 145.8 cm long; bookcase, 210.8 cm high × 66.6 cm wide × 41.3 cm long; chest of drawers, 93.2 high × 102.6 wide × 41.3 long■

2. Cot from the natural series from Bebeform■
Manufactured in chestnut with hand carved decorative details. A drawer is included in the base. Natural non-toxic finishes. Dimensions: 78.6 cm wide × 138 cm long■

3, 4 and 5. Painted cots from Bebeform■
Cots with various amusing infantile motifs hand-painted in water-based paints. A practical drawer is incorporated in the base of all models. Dimensions: 78.6 cm wide × 138 cm long■

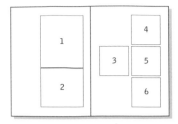

1. Cot "Eleoco'" from Cyrus Company▪

Cot with metal frame and fabric covering that can be detached and washed▪

2. The furniture range and fabric accessories "Malva" from Fuli & C. ▪

The principal motif in this group is the flower and it is repeated as much in the fabrics as in the pieces of furniture which leads to the creation of a totally coordinated atmosphere▪

3, 4, 5 and 6. Cots from the natural series from Bebeform▪

These cots are made of solid chestnut and each one includes a practical container drawer in its base. Here, one of the main characteristics is the application of artisanal techniques such as the hand carved animals. Finishes are in natural non-toxic products. Dimensions: 78.6 cm wide × 138 cm long▪

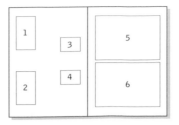

1. Wardrobe from the "DOG SET" series from Bebeform▪
The surfaces and corners are finished by hand. The drawers slide over metal runners. The reliefs are hand-carved. Dimensions: 173 cm high × 93 cm wide × 56 cm long▪

2. Wardrobe from the "BEAR SET" series from Bebeform▪
Hand-finished surfaces and corners. Includes three drawers with metal runners, two large shelves and a bar to hang clothes. The bears are carved by hand. Dimensions: 190 cm high × 98 cm wide × 53cm long▪

3. Chest of drawers from the collection "DOG SET" from Bebeform▪
Also manufactured with only four doors. Inside, there are drawers and an adjustable shelf. Dimensions: 87 cm high × 138 cm wide × 52 cm long. ▪

4. Chest of drawers from the "CAT SET" series from Bebeform▪
The entertaining decorative elements in the form of cats are carved by hand using artisanal techniques. As the rest of the series, this piece has a high quality non-toxic finish. Dimensions: 88 cm high × 138 cm wide × 53 cm long▪

5 and 6. Two possible combinations of the "KOC" model from Perelló▪
Both combinations include decorative baskets, which fulfil the function of drawers, and handles in the form of moons. Dimensions: cot, 60 ×120 cm or 70 × 140 cm; chest of drawers, 94 cm high × 110 cm wide × 55 cm long; wardrobe, 174 cm high × 110 cm wide × 55 cm long▪

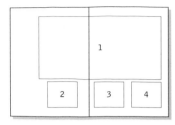

1. Baby's room from the "MAPPA-
MONDO" collection from Assomobili.
This collection is notable for its modular nature that allows it to be assembled in many different ways. The
cot "SIRIO" along with the bath-
changer can be converted into a bed,
small desk - adjustable in height -
and bedside table or set of drawers.
2, 3 and 4. Chest of drawers from
the firm Bopita.
The furniture from this firm offers
many possibilities as far as colors
and decoration is concerned. The
illustrations are hand-painted and
have been designed by Yvonne
Jagtenberg.

The following pages:
The "TAFF" furniture collection from
Hülsta.
This room features bright colors and
natural sycamore. The cot has bars
on one side and a round transparent
acrylic window on the other. The mattress base can be adjusted to five different heights to adapt to the child's
growth.

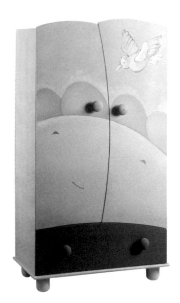

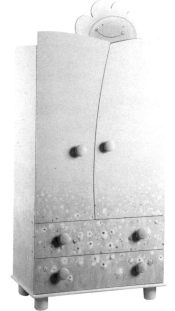

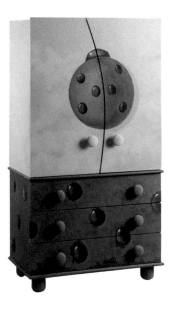

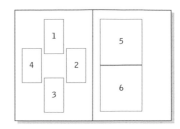

1, 2 and 4. Painted wardrobes from Bebeform■

All of the pictures are painted by hand using water-based paints. Hand-painted furniture introduces a personal and colorful note into child's room■

3. Wardrobe from the firm Bopita■ Available in different combinations of colors and designs. The illustrations, based on a design by Yvonne Jagtenberg, are painted by hand■

5. Bath from the "TRANVÍA" collection from Micuna■

Due to its versatility, this is a very practical piece of furniture. In addition to being a chest of drawers and bath, it also fulfils the function of changer. It is manufactured in pine and stained to a fir wood color or in green. Dimensions: 88 cm high × 78 cm wide × 49 cm long■

6. Bath with matching fabric "CARTUJA" from Babymobel■

Bath and changer made in chestnut stained pine. The ceramic accessory is hand-painted. Dimensions: 88 cm high × 78 cm wide x 49 cm long■

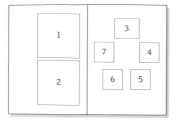

1. Chest of drawers and clothes rail from Cyrus Company▪

Incorporated in the chest of drawers are some decorative elements in natural wood in the form of silhouettes of bears▪

2. Chest of drawers and changing table from the "Rêve" collection from Jacadi. ▪

Both pieces are manufactured in pine stained in a honey color. The doors contain Plexiglas windows that include fixtures from which curtains may be hung. Dimensions: 84 cm high × 100 cm wide × 54 cm long. The changing table measures 90.5 cm in width▪

3, 5, 6 and 7. Chests of drawers from Bebeform▪

Chests of drawers in different designs made in natural materials and which include hand-painted designs. These are combined with wardrobes and cots to introduce a touch of nature into the baby's room▪

4. Chest of drawers from the collection "Funky Fairies" from Heather Spencer Designs▪

Manufactured in MDF and hand-painted with non-toxic paints. The figure is cast in resin from a carved original. Dimensions: 75 cm high × 81 cm wide × 46 cm long▪

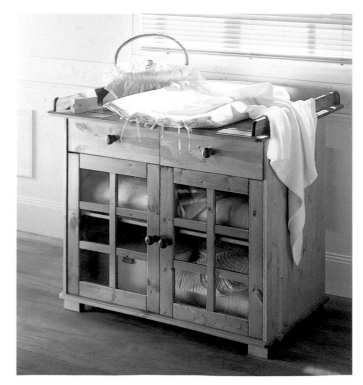

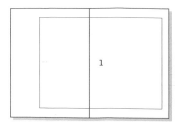

1. Furniture from the "HAVANNA"
collection from Bébé-Jou.
A timeless design that combines
pine with the wickerwork fronts of
the hanging drawers. Dimensions: cot,
60 × 120 cm or 70 × 140 cm; chest
of drawers, 95 cm high × 120 cm
wide × 53 cm long; wardrobe,
190 cm high × 144 cm wide × 55 cm
long; shelf with drawer, 67 cm high ×
48 cm wide × 25 cm long.

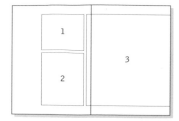

1. Collection of bedclothes "WENDY" and wickerwork hanging cradle from Leipold▪

2. Chest of drawers – changing table with plastic treated fabric from the collection "WENDY" from Leipold▪

3. During the first months of the baby's life, the most habitual is to find the baby's cot along side the parents' bed. This bedroom stands out for its luminosity and for a certain air of romantic nostalgia found in the antique furniture combined with soft colors▪

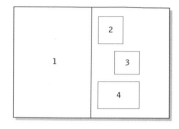

1. Furniture from the "LOUVRE" co-llection from Bébé-Jou∎
The soft blue tones with small details in red from the "SLEEPY" fabric se-ries provide a background for this apparently simple furniture that combines white with the natural wood finishes. Dimensions: cot, 60 × 120 cm or 70 × 140 cm; chest of drawers, 89 cm high × 110 cm wide × 55 cm long; wardrobe, 178 cm high × 130 cm wide × 55 cm long∎

2 and 3. Fluffy toys from the firm Bopita∎
These amusing fluffy toys can also be used as cushions. The animals owe their inspiration to designs by Yvonne Jagtenberg∎

4. Cushions from the collection "CONEJITOS POM-POM" from Tirimil-itín∎
Comfortable cushions in neutral tones decorated with amusing em-broidered bunny rabbits∎

The following pages:
Furniture collection from the "HI-MALAYA" line from the firm Tartine et Chocolat∎
The intense combinations of colors along with the reliefs that decorate the different pieces attribute to this room the feeling that it has just ap-peared from a fairy tale∎

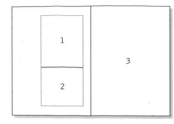

1. Wooden horse from Jacadi. ■
This toy, which is typically passed from father to son, is of a design that will never fall out of fashion. Dimensions: 50 cm high × 35 cm wide × 78 cm long■

2. Padded chair and carpet from the "LE REINE DES GRENOUILLES" collection from Jacadi■
The chair is made from an interior foam frame with a removable 100% cotton fabric cover. The carpet is made of a hand washable velvet cotton. Carpet measurements: 170 cm wide × 110 long■

3. For the more creative and those with artistic talent, the walls in this room for children become a blank canvas which gives free rein to the imagination to create unrepeatable designs to stimulate the senses of the newborn baby and provide a warm and colorful atmosphere. An adequate illumination will help strengthen the effect of intimacy and warmth■

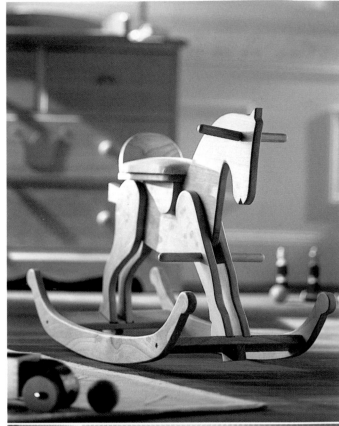

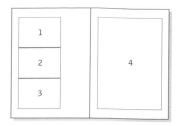

1. Furniture collection "GINEBRA" from Mobilín▪

The practical convertible cot, which represents a basic piece of furniture in the baby's room, changes over the years and becomes an essential element within the youngster's room▪

2. The "MONACO" furniture collection from Mobilín▪

As in the previous room, the convertible cot stands out along with the carefully chosen matching colors. The cot converts into a junior bed and sifonier. Cot measurements: 80 × 185 cm (not including sifonier)▪

3. Cot "CONVER" from Micuna▪

Cot manufactured in pine that transforms along with the growth of the child. By adding some simple accessories, it can be converted into a large bed, a bedside table, into a table with shelves, into a bookcase and even into a toy tent▪

4. Cot from the "MAPPAMONDO" collection from Assomobili▪

Both lacquered sides of the cot can be detached to make an individual bed. The wall panel is also lacquered and contains shelves▪

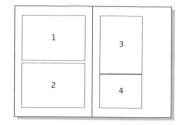

1. Furniture from the "ALASKA" collection from Mobilín.
A range lacquered in white which is fully capable of blending in with any surroundings. The convertible cot, which due to its various different pieces adapts to the child's development, stands out.

2. Padded chair and carpet from the "RUBAN" collection from Jacadi.
The chair, in a sandy color, is upholstered in removable 80% cotton and 20% polyester fabric. The carpet is in hand-washable cotton velvet. Carpet measurements: 110×110 cm.

3. Decorative accessories from the "LES FÉES" collection from Jacadi.
In this atmosphere of pink tones all of the elements, from the fluffy toys to the doll's cot in wickerwork with beech frame and *chambray* covering, match perfectly. The cotton based velvet carpet measures 110×110 cm.

4. Stimulation carpet with arches from the "CRABES ET COQUILLAGES" collection from Jacadi.
This carpet includes all sorts of accessories to stimulate the baby's senses. It is machine washable. Dimensions: 100×100 cm.

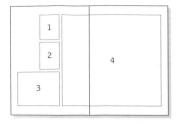

1. Carpet from the "TINA & TIN" collection of decorative accessories from Tirimilitín■
2. Carpet from the "CONEJITOS POM-POM" collection from Tirimilitín■
This decorative article forms part of an extensive collection that includes a large number of accessories able to transform the appearance of any child's room■
3. Cot and color coordinated fabrics from the "VENUS" collection from Fuli & C■
In this range, the star has been chosen as a predominate motif and it has been combined with delicate tones in whites and nature colors■
4. Range of furniture of the "ZIDANE" model from Bébé-Jou■
The sliding doors and drawers with etched glass fronts offer a differentiating touch. Dimensions: wardrobe, 190 cm high × 120 cm wide × 57 cm long; chest of drawers, 93 cm high × 120 cm wide × 55 cm long■

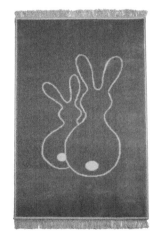

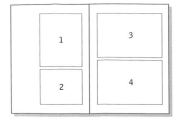

1. Cot and set of bedclothes from the "Nube" collection from Babymobel▪
2. Cot from the "Funky Fairies" collection from Heather Spencer Designs▪
Manufactured in MDF and hand-painted with non-toxic paints. The figure is cast in resin from an original carving. Dimensions: 99 cm high × 82 cm wide × 145 cm long▪
3. Cot and changer from the "Sleepi" collection, design by Grønlund and Knudsen for Stokke▪
Furniture manufactured in beech. The base of the cot can be set at four different heights. One of the sides of the cot can be detached so that the child can get in and out on his or her own once he or she is older. The cot may also be converted into two chairs or a child's bed▪
4. A group from the "Noche" collection from Micuna▪
This furniture is manufactured in natural Scandinavian fir wood and the decorative details are stained in green▪

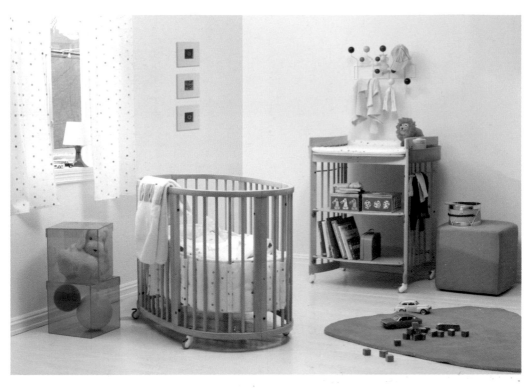

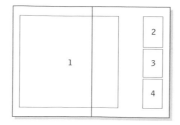

1. A group from the "EUGENIA" collection from Micuna.
This atmosphere transmits an unmistakable sensation of romanticism. The furniture is made in pine with a soft scaling finish in white. An optional drawer is available for the cot.
2. Cot "SLEEPI MINI". Design from Grønlund and Knudsen for Stokke. This small cot converts into the baby's first bed. Measuring no more than 67 cm in width, it fits through any door and is easy to move from one room to another.
3. Hanging wickerwork cradle with veil model "RHODOS" along with a set of bedclothes from the "LANDHAUS" collection. From Leipold.
4. Wickerwork cradle "BARBAROSSA" which comes complete with covers for the eiderdown, pillow, mattress and metal support. The bedclothes are from the "LEUCHTSTERN" collection. From Leipold.

The following pages:
The "LUCA E DANIELE" collection from Pasito a Pasito.
This collection combines all sorts of articles in fabrics and decorative accessories in which smooth surfaces in beige tones are matched with details from a lively checked pattern. The accessories, in addition to being highly decorative, cover all of the baby's necessities.

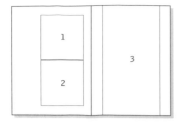

1. Luminous garland and clothes rack from the collection "LE REINE DES GRENOUILLES" from Jacadi▪
The garland has been hand-adorned with petals in the form of a small bell and transmits a feeling of great warmth. 20 electric light bulbs have been incorporated and the overall length is 3.1 m. The clothes rack is in lacquered wood and has a height of 118.5 cm▪

2. The highchair with tray "DELTA" from Mobilín▪
The seat and footrest are adjustable in height enabling the highchair to grow with the child▪

3. Luminous garland, ruler and cushioned seat from the collection "CRABES ET COQUILLAGES" from Jacadi▪
The garland is made up of amusing marine animals. The ruler is in MDF painted by hand with a height of 138 cm. The seat is upholstered in a removable fabric of a denim color▪

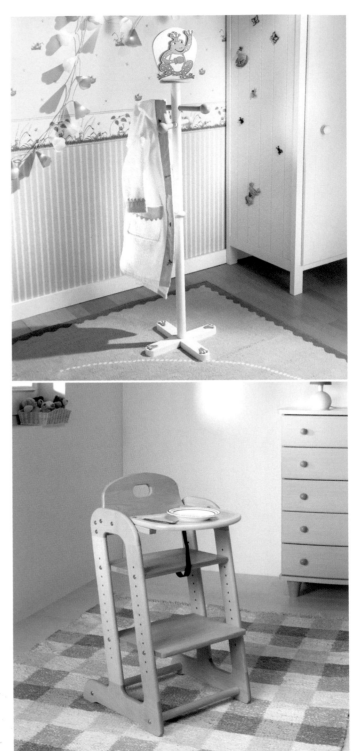

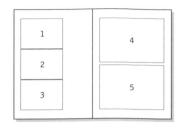

1. Eiderdown and polar BLANKET from the collection "CRABES ET CO-QUILLAGES" from Jacadi.
The blanket measures 76 × 104 cm and the eiderdown 90 × 140 cm.
2. Activity water lily from the collection "LE REINE DES GRENOUILLES" from Jacadi.
This stimulation article can be attached to the cot or to the playpen.
3. Changer with mat in plastic-covered fabric branding the "SEREN-GETI" pattern from Leipold.
4 and 5. Two possible arrangements for the "BRUSELAS" model from Mobilín.
The elements of this model can be arranged in many different ways and they are also available in a great variety of finishes. Dimensions: cot, 60 × 120 cm; wardrobe, 180 cm high × 117 cm wide × 63 cm long; chest of drawers, 85 cm high × 108 cm wide × 50 cm long.

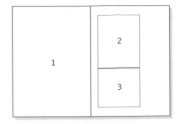

1. A selection of furniture from the collection "PETITS AMIS SAPIN" from Tartine et Chocolat∎
The honey-colored finish, carved initials and attractive check transmit a warm atmosphere reminiscent of that furniture of a solid character typically found in old noble country homes, but with a contemporary finish and comfort∎

2. The "RAPHIA" model from Jacadi∎ Cot and small table with MDF frame lacquered in white. The small chair is in solid pine. The mattress base is in beech and can be set at two different heights. Dimensions: cot, 66 × 126 cm; small table, 51.5 cm high × 44 cm wide × 64 cm long; small chair, 56 cm high × 27 cm wide × 30 cm long∎

3. Pieces of furniture and fabric articles from the "SEESTERN" collection from Schardt∎
Furniture made in beech with central doors in Plexiglas with decorative etchings in the form of stars and seashells. The same design is repeated in the fabric accessories∎

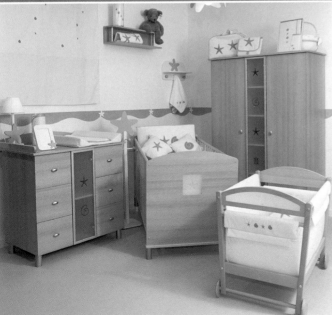

1. Room with furniture from the "TOLEDO" collection from Bébé-Jou∎ This collection, made in beech, stands out for the modern style transmitted as much by its metallic handles as by the combination of white and lavender, the height of its legs and its purity of form. Available in alternative color combinations. Dimensions: wardrobe, 200 cm high × 110 cm wide × 60 cm long; chest of drawers, 95 cm high × 110 cm wide × 55 cm long; cot (convertible into child's bed), 60 × 120 cm or 70 × 140 cm∎

2 and 3. Decorative table lamps that match the rest of the articles from the "CONEJITOS POM-POM" and "TINA & TIN" collections from the firm Tirimi-litín∎

4. Ceiling lamp and small chair that form part of the entertaining collection of decorative accessories "CA-RAMEL" from Pasito a Pasito∎

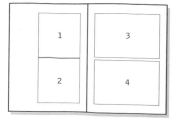

1. Stimulation carpet from the collection "Au Pays de la Savane" from Jacadi.
The playpen can be adapted. Numerous activities with a diversity of sounds are included.

2. Playpen and doll's cot from the collection "Ruban" from Jacadi.
The playpen is in lacquered pine and can be folded. The doll's cot is in wickerwork and the frame and wheels in beech. Dimensions playpen: 59 cm high × 92 cm wide × 100 cm long.

3. Composition from the collection "Mark" from Paidi.
The frame of this furniture is in solid beech while the frontal panels are available in sycamore or wickerwork. Dimensions: wardrobe, 184.7 cm high × 133.4 cm wide × 55 cm long; chest of drawers, 87.7 cm high × 92.2 cm wide × 46.9 cm long.

4. Room with furniture from the "Trésor" collection from Jacadi.
All of the furniture is in solid pine stained in a honey color. The wardrobe, the cot and the table are a l l collapsible. Dimensions: wardrobe, 191 cm high × 104 cm wide × 55 cm long; table, 50 cm high × 44 cm wide × 64 cm long.

The following pages:
Cot and small bench from the collection "Henry's Hideaway", design from Amanda Heath for Wigwam Kids.
One of the sides can be detached to convert the cot into a small bed or elegant sofa. A practical drawer has been included in the base. Dimensions: cot, 110 cm high × 69 cm wide × 150 cm long; bench, 45 cm high × 70 cm wide × 30 cm deep (photo: Mark Seager, The Picture House UK).

As of this age, the room should offer a facility for transformation and a multiplication of functions. The idea of versatility must be present in the majority of choices given that the room ceases to be simply a place to sleep and becomes a multifunctional space that should allow freedom in which to play, to do homework comfortably, to create hundreds of works of art or to entertain friends.

With age, the small one's possessions also multiply. In which case, finding a solution to the problem of having enough space to store things tends to be the main challenge that has to be faced. Everything should have its place: clothes, toys, school things, books, the collections of everything imaginable (dolls, stones, tractors, comics, marbles...)

In addition, everything has to be organized in such a way that the child can maintain an order over his or her belongings. This is to say, position the clothes bar in the wardrobe at the child's level, the drawers, the shelves and chests or toy storage boxes in such a way that he or she has easy access to his or her toys and clothes (in this way, a dangerous necessity to climb can also be avoided). As the child grows, the furniture in the room may be changed in height or repositioned.

During these years, children begin to develop their own personalities, characters and tastes. Therefore, it is important to allow them to participate in the decoration of their rooms in such a way that enables them to feel that these spaces are completely their own. After all, they will be the ones who spend the major part of their time there. In addition, the way they play with light along with their creative manipulation of space can lead to some surprising results. Without a doubt, should their choice of colors clash drastically with our own taste, ideally, we should come to a "friendly

agreement" to tone the colors down a little or aim to achieve this by introducing suitable accessories into the room. On the other hand, the child's hobbies and interests can lead to some highly decorative results. If he or she is crazy about fluffy toys, drawing or toy cars, shelves can be arranged to exhibit the collections which, at the same time, imposes an order over these elements.

Security is also very important at this stage. It is now when children dive headfirst into a discovery of the world with an endless curiosity and, generally, an almost absent sense of danger. Statistics show that the majority of accidents take place in the home. It is therefore necessary to minimize the risks by putting into practice all of the precautions within our reach. Security depends, fundamentally, on our common sense (keep the room free of anything that can cause harm such as small objects that can be swallowed, furniture that can easily fall over or carpets that slide and can provoke falls) and on the use of articles that increase protection from accidents such as protectors for electrical plugs and for the sharp corners of tables, or the installation of barriers in doorways and at the top of the stairs, for example. Whatever the case, we should remember that each stage of our children's development requires a particular series of precautions.

The challenge is to achieve, based on the collaboration between parents and child, an environment that is imaginative, safe, practical, flexible and pleasing and that transmits energy and a feeling of calmness at the same time. The overall result of the light and color combined with appropriate furniture will lead to harmonious and stimulating surroundings in which our children will be able to grow according to their necessities.

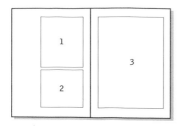

1. Bed "Eleoco'" from the Bambino collection from Cyrus Company∎ Romantic bed with canopy. The mattress base is made of slatted wood over a metal frame∎

2. Chest of drawers and mirror with small drawer from the children's collection from The White Company∎ Articles manufactured in MDF with a soft lacquered finish. Dimensions: chest of drawers, 91 cm high × 87.5 cm wide y 42 cm long; mirror, 52 cm high × 38 cm wide y 14.5 cm long∎

3. Small sofa "Trecasseti" from the collection for children from Cyrus Company∎ The frame is in polyurethane and the upholstery is removable and washable∎

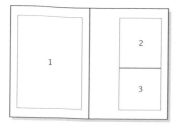

1. Buck beds with decorative elements from The Children's Furniture Company∎
The buck beds are manufactured in natural beech and fulfill all ecological and security requirements. They can also be used as two individual beds. Dimensions: 171 cm high × 106 cm wide × 200 cm long∎
2. Child's bed with two drawers from the collection "Trésor" from Jacadi∎ Manufactured in solid pine with drawers on metal roller runners. Dimensions: 89 cm high × 95.2 cm wide × 202 cm long∎
3. Four-drawer chest of drawers from The Children's Furniture Company∎
Manufactured in natural beech from controlled forests. Available in various colors and finishes∎

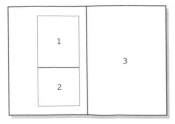

1. Furniture from the "RAPHIA" collection from Jacadi■
Made in MDF and finished with two coats of white lacquer. Complies with European pediatric regulations. The former cot has been converted into a child's bed apt for children up to six years old. The top of the wardrobe can be opened. Dimensions wardrobe: 173 cm high × 75 cm wide × 47.5 cm long■
2. Range of furniture from the "SPLASH" collection from Heather Spencer Designs■
The furniture is manufactured in MDF and hand painted using non-toxic materials. The characters are in resin casts. Dimensions: bed, 102 cm high × 98 cm wide × 200 cm long; chest of drawers, 91.5 cm high × 112 cm wide × 53.5 cm long; toy chest, 43 cm high × 88 cm wide × 37.5 cm long■
3. Room decorated with furniture from the "HIMALAYA" collection from Tartine et Chocolat■
Wooden furniture lacquered with products that fulfill all pediatric security requirements in force. The canopy incorporated in the bed gives the atmosphere an exotic and romantic air■

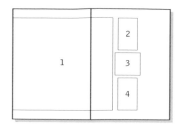

		2
1		3
		4

1. Furniture from the collection "CIRCUS" from Heather Spencer Designs. Good fun is guaranteed with these cheerful and colorful designs. Made in MDF and hand painted. The circus characters are resin casts.

2. Wardrobe from the "JUNGLE" series from Heather Spencer Designs. In the same way as the rest of the collection, this wardrobe is manufactured in MDF. The friendly jungle animals are painted by hand. Dimensions: 154.5 cm high × 95 cm wide × 53.5 cm deep.

3. Chest of drawers from the collection "PETS" from Heather Spencer Designs.

In this collection, the decorative elements in resin represent entertaining domestic animals. Dimensions: 91.5 cm high × 112 cm wide × 53.5 cm long.

4. Bookcase from the collection "CHILDREN'S PINE" distributed by Somethingspecial.

Manufactured in solid pine. Incorporates letters carved in relief that can be personalized.

The following pages:

1. Beds from the "SHUTTER" range with moons and stars cut out of the wood. The wicker basket is the "WEDNESDAY" model from Finn & Hattie.

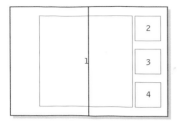

1. Room with a marked rural air which is reflected as much in the rough treatment of the walls as in the decorative accessories in a classical and rustic style or in the straw hat. In this case, the touch of color comes from the hand on the bedclothes∎

2. Table and chair from The Children's Furniture Company∎
Manufactured in solid beech and with rounded corners. The chair consists of four pieces that are held together with the help of just one peg and is suitable for children up to the age of seven. Dimensions table: 53 cm high × 55 cm deep∎

3. Shelf painted in blue from The Children's Furniture Company∎
Combines beech with stainless steel bars. The engraved designs match the rest of the furniture from this firm. Dimensions: 61 cm high × 80 cm wide × 24 cm long∎

4. Chair "PETER" designed by Hans J. Wegner. Produced by Carl Hansen∎
This design is more than 100 years old and continues to be completely contemporary. The pieces can be assembled without the use of any tools, which means that in addition to being a chair, it becomes a construction toy for the child. Dimensions: 47 cm high × 42 cm wide × 32 cm long∎

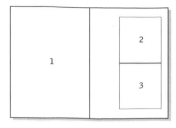

1. Bed with trundle lacquered in white from the collection for children from The White Company▪
Manufactured in MDF and available in two sizes and in various colors. Dimensions of individual bed, that allows for another bed to be stored below: 92 cm high × 101 cm wide × 202 cm long▪
2. Set of bedclothes "STARS" from The White Company▪
This bed set is made in 100% cotton with small embroidered stars▪
3. Bedspread "RED STAR" made in 100% cotton with amusing stars and colorful hand-embroidered trimmings. From the collection for children from The White Company▪

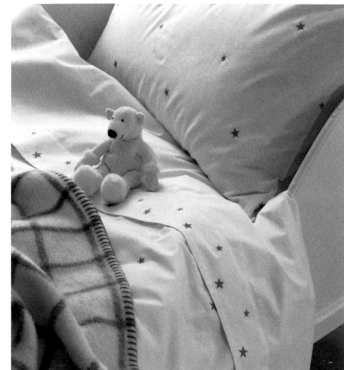

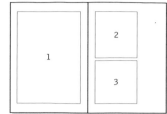

1. Room decorated with articles from the "COQUILLAGE GRIS" collection from Tartine et Chocolat.
The soft pearl color of this furniture along with the matching accessories creates a tranquilizing and harmonious atmosphere.
2. Dolls' house from The White Company.
This dolls' house can also be used as a shelf. It is manufactured in MDF with a soft white finish. Dimensions: 129 cm high × 111 cm wide × 30 cm deep.
3. Bedside table from the collection created by The Children's Furniture Company.
The upper drawer is available in a carved or plain version. Dimensions: 64 cm high × 38 cm wide × 38 cm long.

The following pages:
Compact element "CASTELLO DI LOT" from the firm Zalf.
Allows for many combinations: bunk beds or overhead bed with study table below, wardrobes... Incorporating the "BENEFIT" system which allows for the upper bed to be lowered to ease bed making.

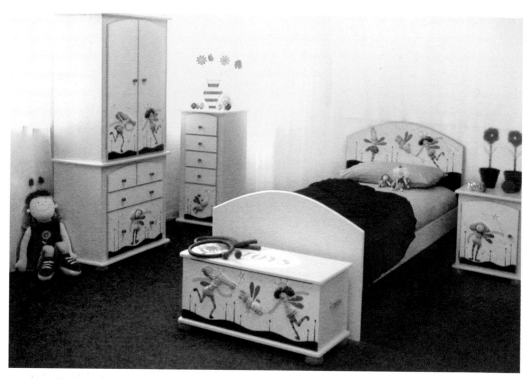

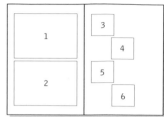

1. Girl's bedroom decorated with furniture from the "FUNKY FAIRIES" collection from Heather Spencer Designs.

This hand-painted furniture is decorated with figures cast in resin that represent fairies from the forest.

2. Bedroom decorated with furniture from Finn & Hattie.

The bed is the "ISLAND BEADBOARD" model and the bedside table and chest of drawers the "NELLIE" model. As all of the furniture is hand-made by craftsmen, customers can choose colors directly. The range has a light rustic appearance of great quality and personality.

3, 4 and 6. Different possibilities in format and design permitted by the collections designed by Heather Spencer Designs.

5. Chest of drawers from Marshmallow Company.

Hand-painted furniture with a delicate design. Various designs and colors can be chosen from. Dimensions: 78.74 cm high × 88.9 cm wide × 53.34 cm long.

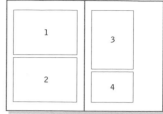

1. Room decorated with furniture and accessories from the collection "My Fairytale" designed by Amanda Heath for Wigwam Kids▪

The combination of this furniture painted in white with the soft pink tones of the cushions and bedclothes converts this environment into a dream world for the small princess (photo: Mark Seager, The Picture House)▪

2. Range of furniture with a marked feminine accent, designed and produced by the firm Cilek▪

3. Bed with canopy "MINICHINA" from the furniture collection for children from Cyrus Company▪

An original bed that includes toy bears that hang from the upper part of the canopy to give an infantile touch▪

4. Furniture with a creative design from the Dutch firm Live and Play▪ The table "CHAMALEON", which includes a practical bag for storing things in the center, is a design from Carla Monchen. The chair "ABEL" is a design from Richard Hutten▪

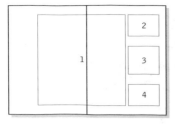

1. Wardrobe and chest of drawers from the collection "NEW ENGLAND". Design from Amanda Heath for Wigwam Kids▪
Furniture made by craftsmen with a timeless design that is suitable for all ages. It creates atmospheres with a lot of personality. (photo: Mark Seager, The Picture House)▪
2, 3 and 4. Various possibilities offered by the cot "SLEEPI" designed by Grønlud and Knudsen for Stokke▪
By incorporating different elements, this cot converts into a bed for an infant, into a sofa or an entertaining toy which will change its form according to the child's imagination and with the help of a Velcro system▪

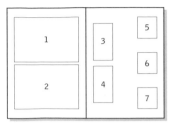

1 and 2. Furniture from the collections "BUGS" and "BEAR" from Heather Spencer Designs∎

Hand-painted furniture with decorative resin elements which represent, with amusing and colorful designs, various themes inspired in the animal kingdom∎

3 and 4. Set of drawers and wardrobe from the collection "PETS" from Heather Spencer Designs∎

The colorful and expressive design of this furniture can transform any space into an explosion of joy, in addition to fulfilling its function of keeping the child's clothes in order∎

5, 6 and 7. Toy chests and bed from the firm Bopita∎

Color is one of the most important elements in the decoration of a child's room. Any one of these pieces of furniture is able to add the necessary dosage to the atmosphere. The friendly hand-painted illustrations are a design from Yvonne Jagtenberg∎

The following pages:
Room composed of bunk beds, wardrobe and study table from Galli∎

All of this furniture is made in oak combined with lacquered panels in lilac. The higher bed includes a curtain that creates a private space∎

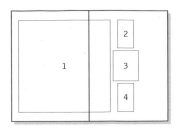

1. Composition from the collection "Sᴡᴇᴇᴛ Hᴇᴀʀᴛ" designed by Amanda Heath for Wigwam Kids■
Una atmósfera bucólica es el resultaA rustic atmosphere is achieved with this combination of pieces of furniture painted in white with amusing cutout hearts and fabric accessories. The metal car in pink, which imitates a vintage style, adds a touch of exclusivity. Dimensions of the bed: 104 cm high × 103 cm wide × 196 cm long (photo: Mark Seager, The Picture House)■

2. Wardrobe from the collection "Cʜɪʟᴅʀᴇɴ's Pɪɴᴇ" distributed by Somethingspecial■
Manufactured in solid pine with designs and letters carved in relief■

3 and 4. Bedside table and set of drawers from the collection "Fᴜɴᴋʏ Fᴀɪʀɪᴇs" from Heaher Spencer Designs■
The bedside table includes a drawer in the interior. Dimensions: bedside table, 60 cm high × 50 cm wide × 46 cm long; set of drawers, 103.5 cm high × 48.5 cm wide × 45 cm long■

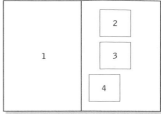

1. An antique metal bed painted white, a mosquito net and colorful blanket are sufficient to create a decor in keeping with the age and personality of this room's young user. Details such as the personalized colored letters on the door or the infantile drawings hanging on the walls contribute to determining this space■

2 and 3. Rocking toys in animal forms from Bopita■

Amusing rocking toys with wooden frames and bodies upholstered in fabric with forms inspired in the designs illustrated in all of the articles from this firm■

4. Rocking toy "HIPPO" designed by Wolfang Rebentisch for Stokke■

Available finished in natural varnish or in a three-toned stain. Recommended as of three years of age. Fulfills European security regulations with regard to children's toys■

The following pages:
This furniture, made to last a lifetime, has been created in oak by Irish craftsmen. Dimensions: bed, 117 cm high × 113 cm wide × 203 cm long; desk, 75 cm high × 135 cm wide × 48 cm long; chest of drawers, 93 cm high × 115 cm wide × 47.5 cm long (photo: Mark Seager, The Picture House)■

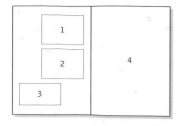

1. Table and chairs in intense colors made in plastic. The chairs have an amusing tomato form. They are from Chicco.

2. Table and chair set from Bopita. Wooden furniture with hand-painted illustrations that imitate a table set for dinner so that it also becomes a toy that stimulates the child's imagination.

3. Table "FROG" and chair "TURTLE" from Live and Play.

These two pieces of furniture are manufactured in different colors and sizes. The seat of the chair can be set at different heights and can also be converted into a table. The holes in the frame allow for up to 30 different decorative combinations.

4. Wardrobe with reversible panels from the "SISTEMA PUZZLE" from Mixel.

This system allows for the maximum use of available space. Numerous accessories can be fitted to the interior of the doors. This model with blackboard doors also offers a highly playful component.

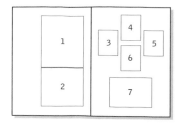

1. The walls and the floor of this room have been converted into surfaces for play. A blackboard and a large roll of paper transforms the walls into large canvases that are waiting to be filled with creativity as is the floor that has become a large games table. The old wardrobe has been painted blue to adapt its image to this recreational area and to provide it with a new function■

2. What stand out in this bedroom are the coordinated fabrics in intense colors which fill the atmosphere of this space with joy. A simple wooden shelf serves as a support for the decorative objects■

3,4 and 5. Stools hand painted with original designs from Marshmallow Company■
Dimensions: 44.45 cm high × 33.65 cm deep■

6. Round hand-painted stool from Marshmallow Company■
Dimensions: 31.75 cm high × 26.67 cm in diameter■

7. Table and stool set from Marshmallow Company■
A set with amusing colorful hand-painted stripes. Dimensions: table, 50.2 cm high × 69.8 cm in diameter; stools, 31.75 cm high × 26.67 cm in diameter■

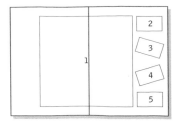

1. This is a good solution for the storage problem that arises as the child grows and, consequently, his or her possessions increase in number. A made-to-measure shelf on which numerous wicker baskets, the content of each being identified with a label, fit turns out to be ideal for keeping everything in perfect order▪
2 and 3. Other first class resources for maintaining toys in order are chests. These two hand-painted models are from the Marshmallow Company▪
Dimensions: 30.5 cm high × 73 cm wide y 38.1 cm long▪
4 and 5. Toy chests from the collections "Bugs" y "Jungle" from Heather Spencer Designs▪
They are made in MDF and painted by hand and include decorative elements made in resin. Dimensions: 43 cm high × 88 cm long × 37.5 cm long▪

The following pages:
Composition from the "Mappamondo" collection from Assomobili▪ The infant's bed is the result of a transformation of the original cot and uses the same headboard and metal frame. The lacquered panel on the wall is for shelves that can be set up in different ways▪

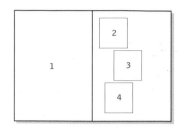

1. The image of an old wooden bed can be completely renewed by painting infantile designs on it. The different colored walls, one of which also contains an amusing design, contribute to the creation of an atmosphere adequate for a child's room■

2, 3 and 4. Beds and chest of drawers from the "CHILDREN'S PINE" collection distributed by Somethingspecial■

Furniture manufactured in solid pine. Includes letters carved in relief that can be personalized■

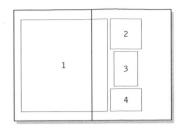

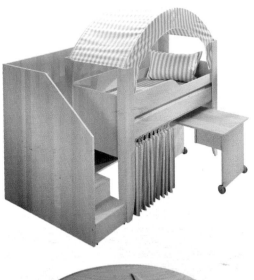

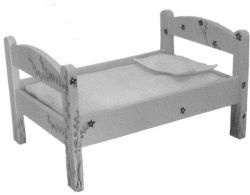

1. Furniture from the collection "Conver" from Babymobel■

The bed with drawers as much as the bedside table manufactured in pine are obtained thanks to a transformation of the original cot of this collection which allows for the furniture to be made the most of during the child's entire growing up process■

2. High bed from the collection "TAFF" from Hülsta■

This modular bed made in sycamore with a natural wood finish is a good way of saving space. The lower part can hold a supplementary bed, a complete bookcase, a desk with drawers or it can be left empty to provide an play area■

3. Solid pine shelf with moons and stars in relief from the collection "CHILDREN'S PINE" distributed by Somethingspecial■

4. An amusing hand-painted bed for dolls or pets from Marshmallow Company■

Dimensions: 29.2 cm high × 36.2 cm wide × 52 cm long■

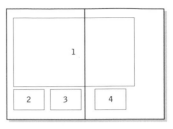

1. Bed for the "PUZZLE" system from Mixel.
Table and chair set hand painted with designs in gold from Marshmallow Company.
Dimensions: table, 55.9 cm high × 68.6 cm in diameter; chairs, 66 cm high × 33 cm wide × 33.5 cm long.
2. Table and chair set hand painted with designs in gold from Marshmallow Company.
Dimensions: table, 55.9 cm high × 68.6 cm in diameter; chairs, 66 cm high × 33 cm wide × 33.5 cm long.
3. Table and chair set painted in amusing colors from Marshmallow Company.
Dimensions: table, 50.16 cm high × 49.53 cm wide × 58.42 cm long; chairs, 56.5 cm high × 26.6 cm wide × 29.2 cm long.
4. Table and chair "LAMA". A contemporary design and daring colors from Live and Play.

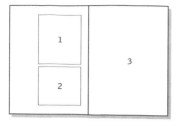

1. Furniture for toys from The Children's Furniture Company.
Made in beech with designs carved on the upper drawer. The interior shelf can be adjusted to allow for large toys to be stored inside. Dimensions: 86 cm high × 96 cm wide × 53 cm long.

2. Table and chair "PETER" designed by Hans J. Wegner. Produced by Carl Hansen.
As these pieces can be assembled without the use of tools, in addition to furnishing, they become construction toys for the child. Dimensions chair: 47 cm high × 42 cm wide × 32 cm long.

3. Upholstered stools "TULLA" and table with rounded forms "LUCILLE" from Finn & Hattie.
This range is well able to personalize and fill any child's room with color. Dimensions: stools, 50.8 cm high × 40.64 cm in diameter; table, 48.26 cm high × 81.28 cm deep.

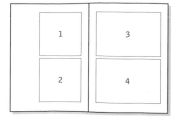

1. Bunk beds "Sʜᴜᴛᴛᴇʀ" from Finn & Hattie▪

The bunks may be disassembled and used as individual beds. Bunk beds are recommended for children as of the age of six▪

2. A group of furniture from the "Oᴄᴇᴀɴ" range from Cilek▪

A modular line with marine motifs that can be arranged in many ways to adapt the room to different ages and necessities▪

3 and 4. Two possible arrangements of the "Dᴇᴅᴀʟᴏ" range from IMA Mobili▪

This modular range in various finishes offers numerous options to maximize the use of available space. Mobile beds that can be moved easily help make the most of the available space that is found beneath a high bed and allow for the installation of a desk, for example. Steps that provide access can be converted into practical drawers▪

The following pages:

Room decorated with furniture from the "Iꜱᴀᴍᴜ" collection from Assomobili▪

This composition with bunk beds and container furniture has been especially designed to save space. The lower bed can be comfortably removed▪

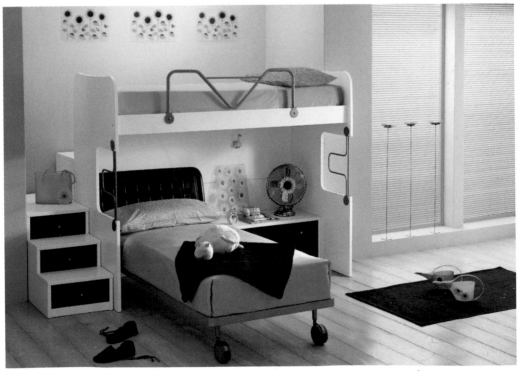

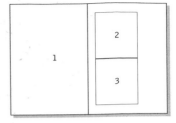

1. A room with a rustic air and some very original built-in bunk beds. Below the lower bed, made-to-measure drawers have been installed to increase storage capacity and practical reading lamps have been fitted over the headboards of each bed■
2. Bunk beds "CROW'S NEST ISLAND" model from Finn & Hattie■
The bunks can be disassembled and used as individual beds. The distance between the two beds is 99.06 cm. Dimensions of each bed: 106.65 cm wide × 205.74 long■
3. Bunk beds from the children's collection from Cyrus Company■
Made with a wooden frame that is lacquered or stained with water-based paints. Some original linen curtains that give intimacy to the small ones and protect from direct sunlight are included■

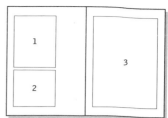

1		
		3
2		

1. Bunk beds from the "CASTELLO DI LOT" program from Zalf▪

This piece of furniture, which is available in various versions, in a single and compact element fulfills a number of different functions: two beds, a shelf and a desk. The lower bed is moved outwards at bedtime▪

2. The "OH! RAZIO DYNAMIC" modular system from Zalf▪

This greatly versatile system allows for the installation of two beds and two desks, which move over metal rails permitting numerous different arrangements, in the reduced space of 270 cm▪

3. Containers "MONOPOLI" and high bed from the "BENEFIT" system from Zalf▪

The mattress base of the high bed can be moved down to ease the task of bed making. The different container modules have been made available in various sizes so as to adapt to the differing necessities of each case▪

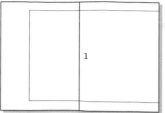

1. Room decorated with furniture from Galli■

The bunk bed "Tʀᴀᴍ" is on castors for displacement and is made in oak with a back panel painted in red. The oak study table and shelves are the model "Aʀɢᴇɴᴛᴏ Vɪᴠᴏ". The bookcase "Qᴜɪɴᴛᴀ" also has a back panel painted in red■

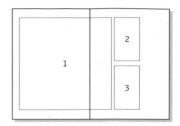

	2
1	3

1. This room, which combines details with a classical air with others of a more contemporary nature, achieves a balanced atmosphere. The bed with the antique mosquito net along with the seat are the elements responsible for introducing a certain touch of nostalgia which contrasts with the treatment of the wall and modern bedside table with castors■

2. Wardrobe from the collection "RÊVE" from Jacadi■

Manufactured in solid pine and finished in a honey color. Two doors with Plexiglas windows, which include a system for hanging curtains, a r e incorporated. The interior shelves can be set at different heights. Dimensions: 162 cm high × 100 cm wide × 46 cm long■

3. Bedside table with drawers from The Children's Furniture Company■ The upper drawer can be engraved with a design chosen by the customer or left completely plain as desired. Dimensions: 64 cm high × 30 cm deep■

The following pages:
Composition from Quelli della Mariani■

An ingenious system of metal rails allows the beds to be moved horizontally to achieve the most comfortable position for each moment. The same system allows for shelves to be set in different positions in the wall panel without having to perforate the wall itself■

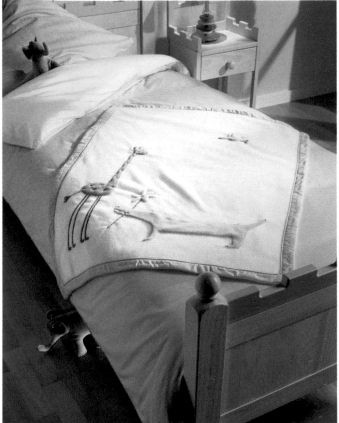

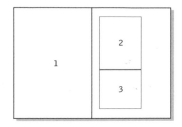

1. A composition that is possible with the "OH! RAZIO DYNAMIC" system from Zalf■

This system is ideal for small spaces as it perfectly integrates two beds and a desk, which can be moved under the bed when not needed, in the same space■

2. Eiderdown set and polar blanket from the "AU PAYS DE LA SAVANE" collection from Jacadi■

Dimensions: Eiderdown case, 140 cm wide × 200 cm long; blanket, 76 cm wide × 104 long■

3. Couch "ISLAND BEADBOARD" from Finn & Hattie■

This piece of furniture can be used as a bed or as a sofa. Dimensions: 105.4 cm high × 205.74 wide × 106.68 long■

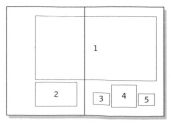

1. Room decorated with furniture from the collection "MAPPAMONDO" from Assomobili▪
This line of furniture is characterized by its capacity to be transformed. The bed, the desk, which can be adjusted in height, and the bedside table are the result of combining the elements from the line's original cot and changer unit▪
2. Hand-painted bench from Marshmallow Company▪
3, 4 and 5. Stools and occasional table hand painted in varying designs from Marshmallow Company▪
Dimensions: table, 45.7 cm high × 58.4 cm deep; stools, 20.32 cm high × 33.65 cm wide × 22.86 cm long▪

The following pages:
Room made up with different pieces of furniture from the firm Galli▪
The two beds with metal frames can be moved along the rails inserted in the wooden panel painted red so that they can be set at various different positions▪

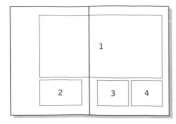

1. Furniture from the "Isamu" collection from Assomobili▪
The bed is the "Enniolo" model and has an original headboard that combines aluminum with strips of wood. The bookcase, with an aluminum frame, is also a desk that can be easily set at different heights without the need of tools, as can be the shelves▪
2. Bed from the "Puzzle" line from Mixel▪
This line offers beds to satisfy all sorts of necessities. Different sizes, materials, finishes or fabric accessories facilitate the existence of a model for each person's taste▪
3. High bed from the "Icaro" collection from IMA Mobili▪
This compact furniture allows a bed, a bookcase and a wardrobe with drawers with sufficient capacity to keep all of a child's clothes in order to fit into the smallest of spaces▪
4. Composition in a boiserie style from Zalf▪
This sort of modular composition is available in many different sizes and can be adapted to almost any situation. It also offers great storage capacity along with trundle kept in a highly reduced space▪

The following pages:
Extreme composition from Galli▪
The daring colors of this room give it a dynamic and creative aspect. The upper bed holds, in its base, a practical container module in intense red and a study table with a surface in natural wood▪

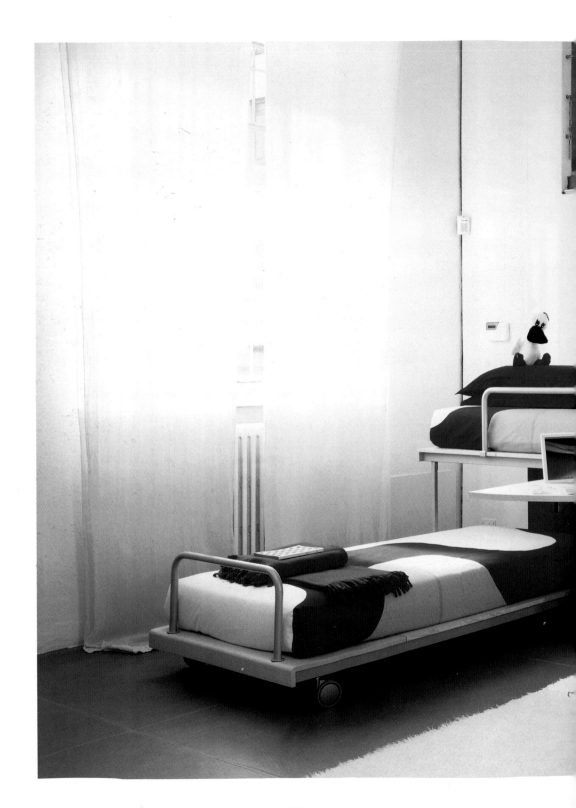

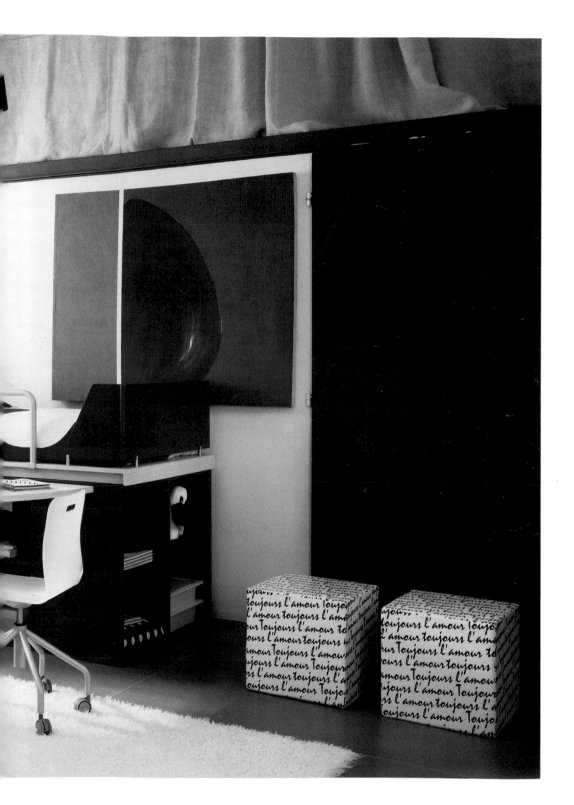

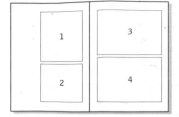

1. High bed from the "CASTELLO DI LOT" system from Zalf▪
This compact system permits various functions to be integrated into only one piece of furniture. In this case, a desk with drawers has been installed under the bed. It could also contain a wardrobe or a combination of both▪
2. Amusing colored modules from the collection "DEDALO" from IMA Mobili▪
In addition to adding a touch of color to the atmosphere, these modules are suitable for holding CD's, books or any other sort of accessory▪
3. Bedroom with furniture from the "DEDALO" collection from IMA Mobili▪
The sliding beds, which move with ease thanks to metal rails, and the wardrobe in a boiserie style manage to make the most of the available space▪
4. Composition from the "ICARO" line from IMA Mobili▪
Two individual beds integrated in a boiserie style wardrobe, conforming to a classical style, have been modernized by the choice of colors▪

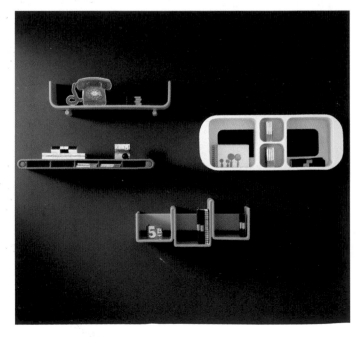

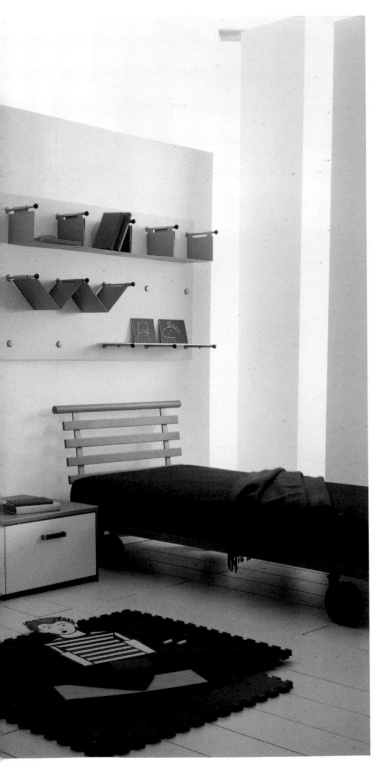

1		
2		4
3		

1. Composition from the "OH! RAZIO DYNAMIC" line from Zalf■
This line allows small spaces to be organized in a dynamic way. The high bed integrates a writing surface that can be hidden under the bed when not in use. The bed slides over another inserted into the space below the bridging wardrobe■

2. Room decorated with various elements from the "ICARO" collection from IMA Mobili■

3. Bedroom composed of furniture from the "MAPPAMONDO" line from Assomobili■
The "CAMPANA" element with a solid wooden frame and finished in cherry-colored melamine allows for the use of a large study area over the bed which is protected by a metallic structure. This structure can also be used as a mattress base for the second bed■

4. Furniture from the "MAPPAMONDO" line from Assomobili■
The bookcase is manufactured with a melamine structure and a lacquered front that incorporates practical glazed doors. The bed with castors is the model "MERCURIO" and over this a lacquered panel into which metal shelves of different shapes are inserted is found■

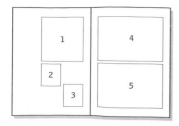

1. The pieces that form "Construction Chair" are assembled as if they
were elements of Mecano. It is a design
from Piet Hein Eek for the firm Live
and Play▪

2. Chair "Sitti" designed by Peter
Opsvik for Stokke▪

Manufactured in beech with an excellent design that allows it to be
most easily adjusted to the size of
the user without the requirement of
tools of any kind. A security bar for
babies is also available▪

3. Chair "EVA DVA" designed by
Sharon and Lawrence Tarantino for
Tarantino Studio▪

This chair possesses the peculiarity
of having been manufactured in
foam. As a result of this, it is not only
very smooth, light and resistant, but
also washable. Available in many col-
or combinations. Its modular design
allows it to be stacked in different
positions▪

4. Study zone composed of furniture
from the "Mappamondo" collection
from Assomobili▪

This composition offers a double
desk manufactured in melamine with
a beech finish and lacquered drawers. The lacquered wall panel allows
for shelves to be hung in various po-
sitions▪

5. Composition from the "Dedalo"
line from IMA Mobili▪

The bridging wardrobe in which the
two beds are integrated allows for a
maximum use of the space available.
The frontal elements lacquered in
red give a certain dynamism to the
atmosphere▪

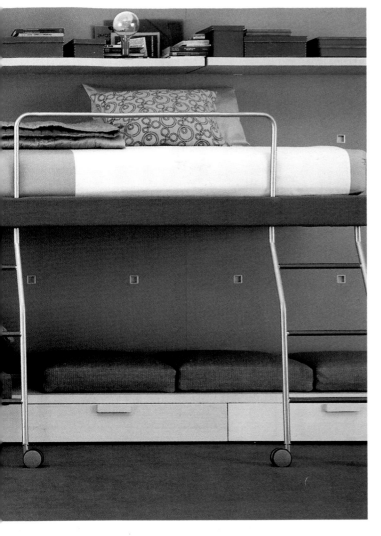

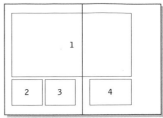

1. Composition from the "PUZZLE" range from Mixel■

The wall panels can be equipped with rails made to measure for the sliding beds to allow the space to be transformed as necessary. The panel can be equipped with up to ten different accessories which allows for the continue renovation of the bedroom. The container drawers, with the help of cushions, convert into a bench■

2. Range "X-MORE" from Cilek■

This range is made up of ten modules which can be arranged in different ways to adapt to the preferences of each user. The design combines aesthetics with an attention for ergonomics■

3. Composition from the "ICARO" line from IMA Mobili■

This modular combination presents a variation from the more classical bunk beds. Not being set one over the other, the two beds create greater dynamism in the atmosphere. The various container modules adjust to the available space■

4. Furniture from the "ICARO" collection from IMA Mobili■

This composition integrates two sliding beds and a desk that can be varied in height, according to the necessities, into a compact module. A practical bookcase with drawers and a built-in wardrobe complete the group■

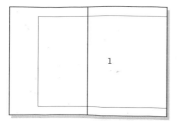

1. Bunk beds "Castello di Lot" from Zalf.
This modular line integrates various functions into a compact unit that optimizes space: two beds, shelves, a study table and drawers all of which, in addition, can be changed into alternative positions. Access to the high bed is by means of the steps at the rear, which also fulfill the function of drawers.

The following pages:
Composition of bunk beds from the firm Galli.
All of the furniture is manufactured in natural oak combined with details painted in red. The beds are on castors for easy moving. The details in orange complete the personalization of the space.

MATURING
LIKES AND
DISLIKES
FALLING IN LOVE
PERSONALIZING
STUDYING

During this period, it seems that children have a desire to leave behind everything related to their infancy as they begin a search for the clothing and environment that will fit their personalities and be suitable for this phase of great change. A new restlessness, demands and necessities begin to appear in the adolescent's life including the need of being able to enjoy a space of his or her own.

As a result, the infant's bedroom becomes a private zone for "personal and exclusive" use. The necessity for intimacy, to have a place to be with friends, speak on the phone, study, listen to music, chat or, simply, relax are the main novelties that arise during these years. The room should be sufficiently adaptable to this life of continual change and transformation.

On occasions, when space is limited, the organization of the available space in such a way that everything has a place can become a piece of delicate engineering given that practical and flexible solutions have to be found to make the most of everything up to the last inch or millimeter. There must be room for a bed (and if there are two, to put up a guest, so much the better); for a wardrobe to keep clothes well ordered (the number of clothes tends to have a direct relationship with age, that is to say, the older the children get, the more clothes they have); for drawers and containers and, of course, an area in which to study.

To satisfy the need for personalization along with that of maximizing the use of available space, over the last few years, manufacturers and designers of juvenile furniture have worked on the development of modular systems that offer not only great compositional freedom, but also an endless number of possibilities when it comes to the moment of adaptation to the space available. They tend to be highly flexible compositions that offer a wide range of sizes, colors and finishes to fit in

with the preferences an adolescent may have. Additionally, it is only necessary to acquire the module needed at any particular time and combine it with the existing furniture. In this way, the room can be completed at the rhythm marked by changing necessities and old infantile furniture becoming obsolete.

An important area in the adolescent's room, where he or she will have to spend more and more time, is the study zone. Therefore, a fundamental factor that should be borne in mind is that of ergonomics. Special attention should be paid to the comfort of the chair and to the table as well as ensuring that the distances between these elements are those recommended so as to avoid incorrect postures. The table should be large enough to provide room for a computer and a writing surface. It is also recommendable to have a bookcase near by so as to have the required books at hand as well as containers to keep music CD's and CD-ROM games for the computer in, not to mention pens and pencils. The area will be completed with an appropriate reading lamp.

In this way, it should be pointed out that there have been a number of important developments in recent years with, for example, the appearance of compact study units that offer many benefits and solutions that make the most of available space as well as offering maximum comfort to the user.

As far as decorative details are concerned, it is evident that at this age the only thing that counts is the personal tastes of each and every child: from the poster of his or her favorite musical group to a collection of postcards, the photos of his or her best friends or a cartoon are some of the things susceptible to be hung on the walls. Unlimited originality and imagination...

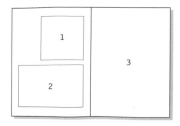

1 and 2. Two possible compositions from the "DEDALO" line from IMA Mobili.
This line of modules allows for an endless number of combinations that can be adapted to the particular necessities of each and every case. In these examples, blue is the predominate color.
3. A combination of elements from various systems designed by Zalf.
The possibility of choosing from among various types of container furniture as well as from alternative desk and bed systems leads to, as a result, a completely personalized room.

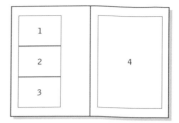

1. Composition of container furniture "Argento Vivo" from Galli▪
The sofa bed with oak frame and drawers painted in white is the model "GRETA". The study table "ON LINE" is also in oak▪
2 and 3. Two proposals from the "SKATE SYSTEM" from Zalf▪
This system combines an excellent functionality with an attractive design in contemporary lines, ideal for older adolescents. It includes innovative elements such as the beds or the diverse models of container furniture▪
4. Composition "OASIS" model from Julia Arredamenti▪
This furniture stands out due to its oriental inspiration. It is made in an ash structure▪

The following pages:
Composition of elements from "CITY LINE" from Doimo▪
This boiserie with bookcase incorporates two metal rails over which the two beds can slide at ease along with the study table, fulfilling, in this way, various functions▪

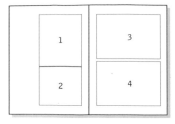

| 1 | 3 |
| 2 | 4 |

1. A highly compact piece of furniture from the "DEDALO" line from IMA Mobili▪

This piece of furniture contains two beds, a writing desk and steps, which also serve as drawers, in a highly reduced space. In this way, the design brings the three main functions of a juvenile bedroom together▪

2. Composition from the "DEDALO" line from IMA Mobili▪

A panel with metal rails acts as a support for two sliding beds and a study table that can be situated one over the other to occupy a minimal space while leaving a large area free to carry out a great diversity of activities▪

3. Proposal from the "ROLLY" line from Erba Mobili▪

A line created for small spaces. The original arrangement allows for a comfortable grouping of two beds, a writing desk that folds into a space below the bed and set of drawers with a front lacquered in an intense lime color▪

4. Composition of modules from the "DEDALO" line from IMA Mobili▪

A complete medium-height wardrobe over which a bed has been situated that is accessed by means of a metal ladder. This solution offers a great storage capacity in a reduced space▪

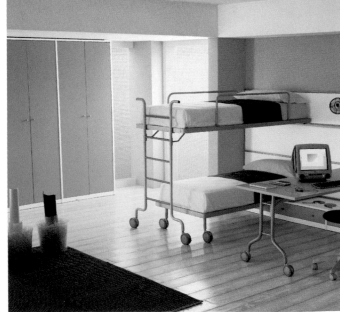

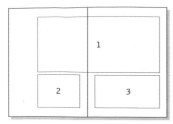

1. Modular furniture "CITY LINE" from Doimo∎
In this composition, the beds are situated in the center of the room creating a defined space that becomes a form of island within the room. The color scheme radiates vitality and luminosity∎

2. Furnishings "ADHOC" from Danona∎
This is one of the many options offered by this line with which it is possible to create spaces molded to any size. The large laminated headboard integrates an original shelf and in itself becomes a support for the bedside table∎

3. Creations from the "TOP DESIGN" program from Benicarló Moble 2000∎
This program stands out for its inspiration in minimalism and for its innovative design, such as the elegant drawers incorporated in the base of the bed or the unusually sized headboard∎

The following pages:
Composition proposed by the firm Galli∎
The outstanding feature of this proposal is the large oak wardrobe which has a module inserted into its side made up of a table and bookcase, which provides a perfectly integrated study area∎

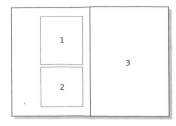

1. Bed with draw from the collection "LIZZIE" from Finn & Hattie.
A nostalgic design for this young-ster's room in which the headboard along with the drawer have an undu-lating relief similar to that of an old washing table.
2. Chest of drawers from the junior program "LOY" from Azcue.
This piece of furniture combines nat-ural ash with drawer fronts lac-quered in orange.
3. Study zone in a rustic style creat-ed by Finn & Hattie.
The shelf and desk with drawers are the "GOOD STUDENT" model and the chair is reminiscent of the classical "WINDSOR" line. A pullout tray for a computer keyboard is hidden behind the central drawer in the table.

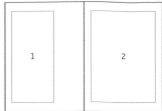

1. Bookcase from the junior program "Loy" from Azcue.
This bookcase has the peculiarity of combining different materials: wooden shelves in ash stained in a beige color, steel bars and a backboard lacquered in an intense blue.
2. Study table "Bay" and chair "Slat" from Finn & Hattie.
The spacious nature of this table allows it to be used for writing as well as for a computer.

The following pages:
Junior room decorated with furniture from the series "Isamu" from Assomobili.
The different pieces in this room combine surfaces in wood stained in cherry with others lacquered in a soft apple green. The writing desk contains a surface that can be pulled out over rails to duplicate the working area.

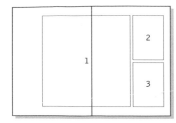

1. Room composed by various elements from the program "Loy" from Azcue■

The furniture from this program is characterized by the way in which it combines ash, whether in a natural finish or stained in beige, with metallic surfaces and details in wicker all of which come together to create a completely balanced atmosphere■

2. Group formed by the table "Porch" and the chairs "Windsor" from Finn & Hattie■

This group is able to create an agreeable zone for table games, a snack or for doing homework in any available corner. Dimensions table: 73.66 cm high × 83.82 cm deep■

3. Furniture from the collection from The Children's Furniture Company■

Manufactured in beech with a natural finish and presented with engraved drawings available in different designs. Dimensions, bed: 97 cm high × 106 cm wide × 200 cm long■

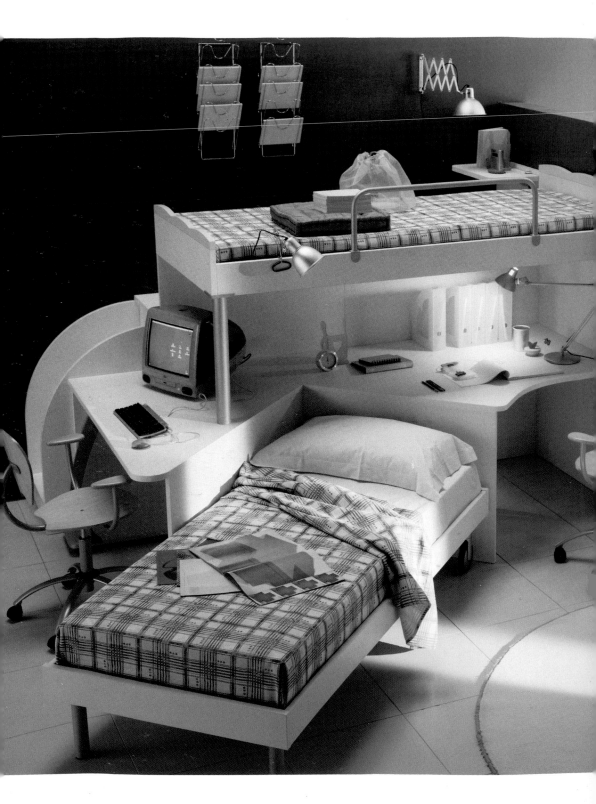

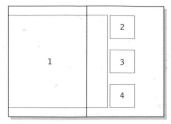

1. Compact piece of furniture from the program "DREAM" from Tieffe▪ This module allows for the integration, in only one block, of two beds and two writing tables that provide the maximum of comfort for their young users and optimize the available space▪

2. Module "NAVIGATOR" from Erba Mobili▪

This compact piece of furniture is a reinterpretation of classical bunk beds which allow for studying and sleeping in one space. A bed and a writing table on castors are situated in the space under the ladder and can be moved or superimposed with nothing more than a simple movement▪

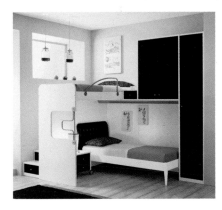

3 and 4. Two possible combinations from the "DEDALO" program from IMA Mobili▪

This program facilitates all sorts of different compositions that allow for a personalization of space in function to the user's necessities and space available as well as offering greater storage capacity or a larger study zone according to preferences▪

The following pages:
Wardrobe system "ALTERNA ROOM" from Zalf▪
In this composition, the wardrobe has folding glass doors. The panel "PICÀ", in the study zone, incorporates metal shelves and a rail onto which a diversity of accessories can be integrated▪

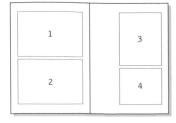

1. Composition with bunk beds from Galli■

Both the lower bed and study surface can be slid under the higher bed to liberate space. The wardrobe in oak contains an original center module, as if it were a window, which can be used as a table or shelf■

2. Furniture program "ADHOC" from Danona■

The bed incorporates an original headboard lacquered in red with shelf and integrated reading lamps. The set of drawers has been lacquered to match the bed■

3 and 4. Vertical folding bed "YALE" from Clei■

Once folded, this bed occupies a space of only 26.5 cm deep and, therefore, can be incorporated into any corner of the home. Dimensions when open: 104 cm wide × 206 cm long■

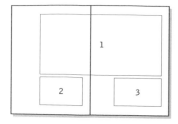

1. Furniture program "TOP DESIGN" from Benicarló Moble 2000▪
This group is made up of a bed and container furniture in various formats characterized for the way in which it combines finishes in natural wood with surfaces lacquered in bright colors and for the purity of line in its design▪

2. Wardrobe from the collection "ROLLY" from Erba Mobili▪
This composition integrates a practical wardrobe with sliding doors that is ideal for maintaining order over all of the adolescent's clothes and accessories▪

3. Composition from the program "Maxi" from Erba Mobili▪
A low element incorporates the writing table and bed. The bed can be moved in all directions while the writing table can be displaced along the length of the metal rail integrated into the piece of furniture which is available in various sizes▪

The following pages:
Composition with the "ON LINE" system from Quelli della Mariani▪
This system takes into account the new necessities generated by the electronic and information technologies and incorporates accessories to allow for the correct storage of the corresponding equipment. The bed can be inserted below the wardrobe to make more space for get-togethers with friends▪

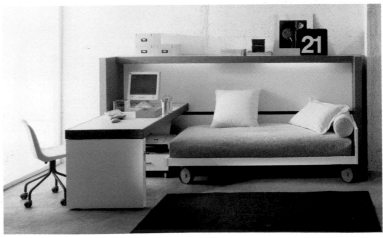

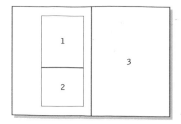

1. Wall container from the "PUZZLE" system from Mixel.
This system is made up from various horizontal and vertical modules that offer great compositional and chromatic freedom and respond to any kind of necessity.

2. Wardrobe from the firm Galli.
This wardrobe, made in oak, integrates in its structure an open bookcase that protrudes beyond the body of the wardrobe increasing its functionality and visual dynamism.

3. Container furniture from the program "PUZZLE" from Mixel.
These sets of drawers with lacquered surfaces form part of a flexible system that includes nine different heights and that lends itself to be painted in intense colors. It incorporates highly original details such as the legs in transparent plastic which are adjustable in height.

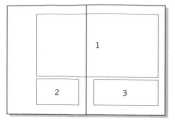

1. Bookcase, bed and bedside table from the program "PUZZLE" from Mixel▪

This program is determined by its great versatility and by its contemporary design that makes the furniture suitable for practically all ages. All of the pieces are available in a great variety of sizes, colors and finishes to provide perfect groups▪

2. Furniture from the program "TOP DESIGN" from Benicarló Moble 2000▪

The container furniture from this program is in simple functional lines and can be arrangement in many different ways so as to adapt to the rest of the bedroom and to the differing necessities of each and every case▪

3. Upholstered bed from the "PUZZLE" program from Mixel▪

This bed is equipped with a folding mattress base in slatted wood that converts the bed into a container with a great capacity which provides valuable storage space▪

The following pages:
Composition from the program "CITY LINE" from Doimo▪

The container furniture lacquered in intense colors and the upholstered bed in lilac create a joyful group that is full of vitality. The writing table and set of drawers have been given wheels so that they can be moved easily▪

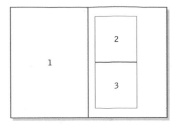

1 and 3. Different tops for study tables from the "PUZZLE" program from Mixel▪

This program offers numerous solutions to make the most of the space available. These surfaces exist in different formats to respond to the necessities of each and every case. They can also be complemented with accessories to create an authentic multimedia corner▪

2. Double computer table from the series "DEDALO" from IMA Mobili▪ This table incorporates an original module that allows the surface to be divided into two equal parts as well as offering more storage space and a practical shelf on which to situate the printer▪

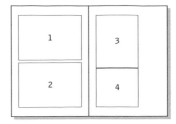

| 1 | 3 |
| 2 | 4 |

1. Study zone from the "On Line" system from Quelli della Marinani. This system can be adapted to the necessities that arise from the use of the new technologies with solutions that create a space for everything. The study table consists of a foldable top that becomes a writing surface.

2. Compositions from the "Oasis" series from Julia Arredamenti.
The furniture pieces combine surfaces in natural ash with others lacquered in a smooth green tone. The bed stands out due to the height of its upholstered headboard.

3. Study module from Erba Mobili. This compact module integrates all of the elements necessary to create a comfortable space in which to study. The table with two tops offers a large work surface and the shelves help maintain all that is necessary close at hand.

4. Integrated bed and study table from the program "Dedalo" from Erba Mobili.
The entire area under the bed has been made the most of to install a complete study zone and, in this way, both functions have been integrated into half the space they would normally fill.

The following pages:
Wall panel "Oh! Razio" and container furniture "Link System" from Zalf.
This panel with metal rails offers great versatility as it allows for many different accessories to be integrated into the system that can be easily changed according to changing necessities.

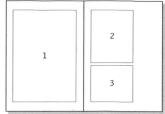

1. A study corner from the "Isamu" system from Assomobili.
The table with an ergonomic form and metal legs includes elements to comfortably house the different pieces of a PC. The bookcase offers great compositional freedom as it can be installed in different positions.

2. Table with integrated shelf from the "Dedalo" program from IMA Mobili.
This module with a metal structure allows for the installation of everything necessary to create a study area in the smallest of spaces.

3. Double study table from the "Dedalo" program from IMA Mobili.
This table with an original design allows for the establishment of two work zones separated by a neutral area. Between the two zones, a shelf has been situated to accommodate all sorts of things used when studying.

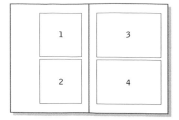

| 1 | 3 |
| 2 | 4 |

1 and 4. Diverse possibilities from the "DEDALO" program from IMA Mobili■

This program is made up of various modules for the study zone with which infinite variations can be created. Shelves or accessories for the computer, in integrated or separate compositions, can be added in function to the space available and/or to the particular demands of each and every case■

2. Writing table from the program "OASIS" from Julia Arredamenti■

Thanks to the independent module in ash that hooks onto the table, this becomes suitable to accommodate a computer as and when necessary■

3. Proposal from the "DREAM" system from Tieffe■

This program is open to many options and combinations. In this case, the surface left free under the ladder has been made the most of to install a study table to which shelves and a computer keyboard tray have been added■

The following pages:

Wall panel system "OH! RAZIO" from Zalf■

By means of this system, all sorts of accessories can be added to the room which can change not only its appearance, but also its functionality with one small movement. The study table is set on metal rails that integrate it into the structure of the panel■

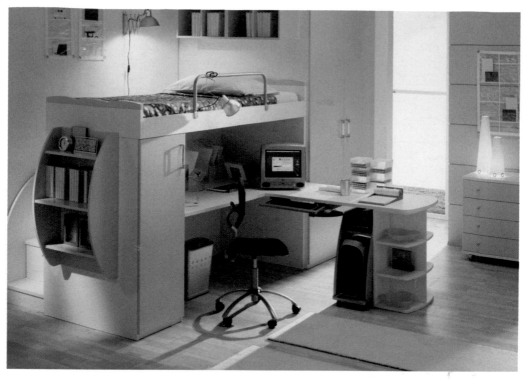

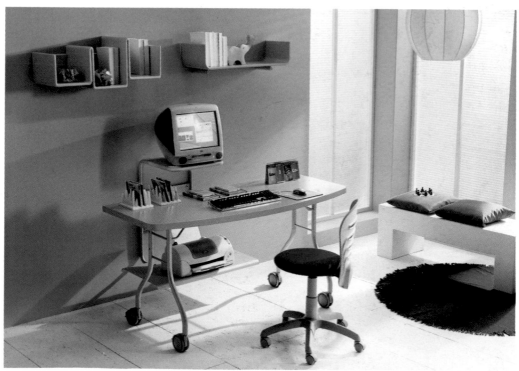

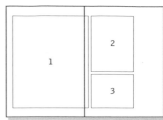

1 and 2. Study zones created with elements from the "SISTEMA ON LINE" from Quelli della Mariani∎
This kind of modular program allows for all sorts of compositions to be created by adding or eliminating elements according to preferences. Its contemporary design, with metal profiles and surfaces in lively tones, adds a touch of youth and color to the room∎

3. Study table from the program "DOMINO 3.1". Design from Francesco Lucchese and Matteo Perego for Di Liddo & Perego∎
This table is made up of two laminated work surfaces with aluminum trimmings that incorporates castors for easy displacement and two rotating shelves that hang from the aluminum column. The study zone is complemented with a set of drawers and with wall panels with container accessories∎

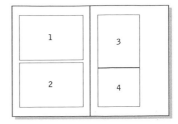

1. Composition from the "ICARO" program from IMA Mobili.
The boiserie style wardrobe contains a sofa bed that allows the room to become a place to get together with friends during the day.

2. Bed with drawers in its base from the "DEDALO" program from IMA Mobili.
This design makes for more storage space so that everything can be kept in its place.

3. Shelf module program "LINK SYSTEM" from Zalf.
The versatility of this program allows for an optimal distribution of the room. The bed "BASIC BED" has an innovative design that transmits the sensation of sleeping in contact with the floor.

4. Furniture program from "ADHOC" from Danona.
This is one of the many options offered by this program with which it is possible to create compositions that adapt to any size and personal taste.

The following pages:
Bedroom from the collection "OASIS" from Julia Arredamenti.
This composition gives off an unmistakable oriental air. The bed sits on a wooden platform that acts as a table in the purest of Japanese styles.

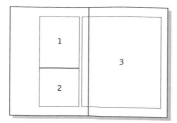

1. Computer table "SURFER" designed by Matteo Perego and Francesco Lucchese for Di Liddo & Perego■

This table is like a trolley with wheels with a tubular aluminum structure and has been specifically designed to work with a computer. Various accessories and extras can be added■

2. Study zone from "SISTEMA ON LINE" from Quelli della Mariani■

The container modules on the wall stand out as a result of the translucent colored glass doors that have been incorporated to keep dirt and dust out■

3. Compact composition from the "ADHOC" program from Danona■

This proposal allows for all of the basics needed for a junior's room to be fitted into a reduced space: study zone, container furniture for storage and, thanks to the sofa bed, a zone for relaxing and getting together with friends■

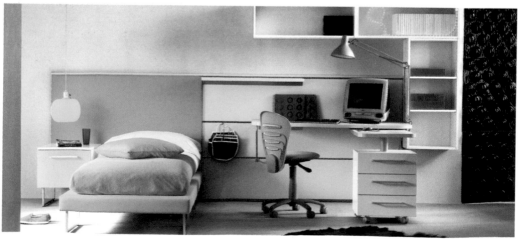

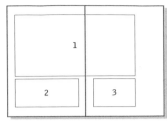

1. A room that has been resolved with elements from the program "SKATE SYSTEM" from Zalf.
The original way in which the bed has been situated in the room along with the shelf just above floor level that supports various pieces of container furniture stand out.

2. Upholstered bed "SKATE" and container modules "MONOPOLI" from Zalf.
Rest and study have both been integrated into this composition that combines various tones of yellow which brings a good dose of vitality to the atmosphere.

3. Composition from the "ALL SIZE" program from Erba Mobili.
This program includes numerous options on beds and desks all of which integrate into this harmonious group thanks to the panel that serves as support for the table and the shelves and is lacquered in the same color as the bed.

The following pages:
Daring composition from the "TOP DESIGN" program from Benicarló Moble 2000.
A certain amount of inspiration in minimalism floats over the atmosphere in this room with furniture of avant-garde design that reflects the latest tendencies in furnishing. The simple bed with wooden base is covered in intense colors that make it stand out in the space.

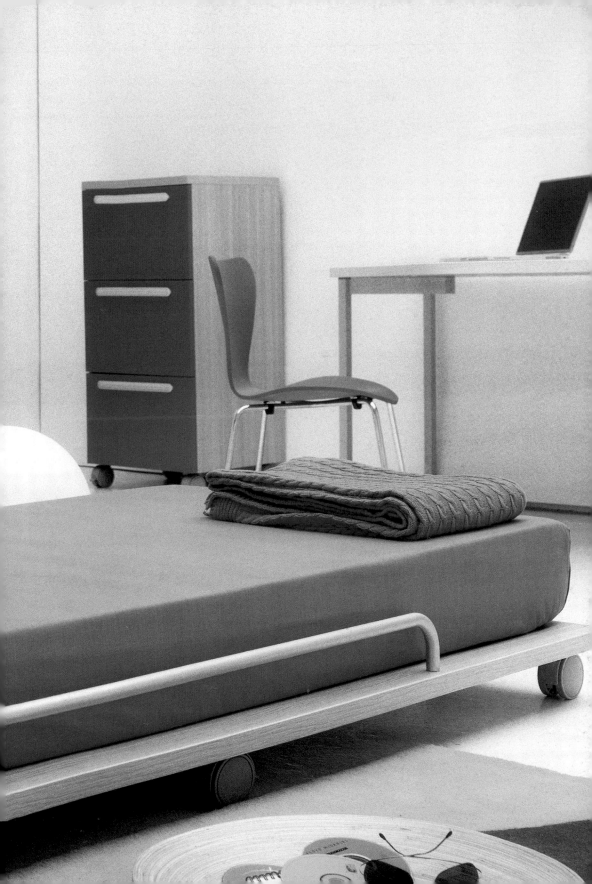

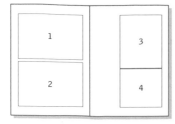

1. Junior bedroom decorated with furniture from the program "Isamu" from Assomobili▪
This composition combines surfaces finished in ash with others that are lacquered in an intense apple green that brings an air of youth to the room. A base containing drawers, also used as a bedside table, supports the bed▪
2. Composition proposed by Zalf▪
This original bed with a wooden structure has its headboard and castors for easy moving integrated into its base. It combines with the wardrobe with folding doors "Alterna" and with the independent study table▪
3. Bunk beds from the system "Domino 3.1". Design from Francesco Lucchese and Matteo Perego for Di Liddo & Perego▪
These functional bunk beds have metal bars incorporated in the headboard area which various container accessories can be hooked on to▪
4. Various solutions for rooms for juniors proposed by Zalf▪
These atmospheres have all been resolved with elements from the modular panel system "Oh! Razio" and container furniture "Monopoli" in matching luminous acid colors▪

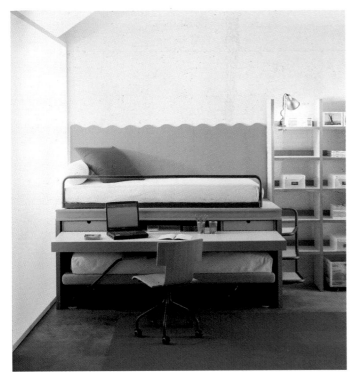

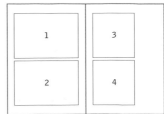

1 and 2. Two possible compositions from the program "DEDALO" from IMA Mobili.

These rooms are characterized by the different solutions they offer for storage and by the way in which different elements with surfaces lacquered in yellow have been combined.

3. Compact furniture from the program "NAVIGATOR JUNIOR" from Erba Mobili.

This program concentrates on solving the problematic presented by small spaces and, in this case, has incorporated two beds and an ample pull out writing table into a space that would normally be fully occupied by only one bed.

4. Composition from "SISTEMA ON LINE" from Quelli della Mariani.

Just one wall is all that is needed to set up these two beds that slide over rails integrated in the wall panel, shelves, a bookcase and study zone.

The following pages:
Elements from the program "SKATE SYSTEM" from Zalf.

The upholstered bed is integrated into the wall panel that is 2.71 m long. Thanks to the metal rails, various accessories, such as these glass shelves, can also be set up on the wall panel.

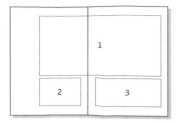

1. Composition from the program "NAVIGATOR JUNIOR" from Erba Mobili.
This proposal offers another good space-saving solution. The second bed is inserted below the wardrobe, which is accessed by the walkway. At bedtime, the bed is pulled out.

2. Furniture from the series "MAPPAMONDO" from Asomobili.
The element "UNIVERSO" satisfies the two main necessities of the junior bedroom when it comes to reduced spaces: a comfortable bed that can be stored under the platform and an extensive study zone that includes a metal protection bar.

3. Possible combination of the system "DOMINO 3.1". Design from Matteo Perego and Francesco Lucchese for Di Liddo & Perego.
The study zone has been installed in the wardrobe so that upon closing the door, it becomes independent from the rest of the room.

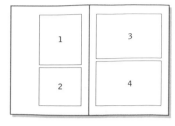

1. Beds and wardrobe from the collection "DEDALO" from IMA Mobili.
Over the lower wardrobes, a platform has been placed to serve as a base to the bed that is pulled out over the lower bed at such a height as to guarantee comfort and make the most of the available space.

2. Composition form the "SISTEMA ON LINE" from Quelli della Mariani.
Group of bookcases, closed container modules and sofa bed that adapt to the changing necessities of the youngster while transmitting a contemporary and colorful image.

3 and 4. Folding beds "BOX" from Clei.
Transformable furniture of this nature units functionality, ergonomics and aesthetics. When the beds are folded up, the room becomes an extensive zone for study and play.

The following pages:
Composition from the program "DREAM" from Tieffe.
A wall panel organizes the room's different functions. The metal rails integrate the bunk beds and study table into the structure and enable them to be moved comfortably. The drawers in the base also serve as a bedside table for the lower bed.

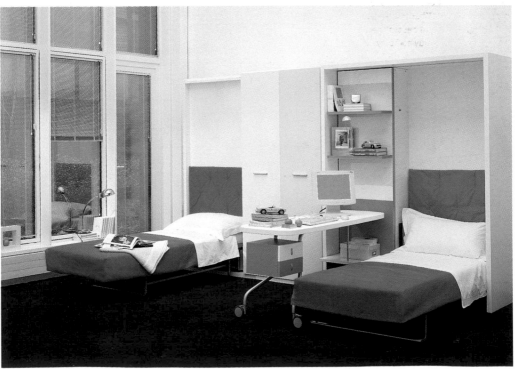

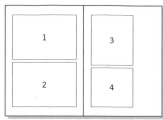

1 and 2. Different compositions from the collection "OASIS" from Julia Arredamenti■
Contemporary aesthetics and details taken from Japanese culture determine these proposals■
3 and 4. Convertible sofa "DOC" from Clei■
This sofa can be transformed into a bunk bed with a latter and security bar through a simple rotation system, which easily allows the transformation. Dimensions sofa: 95 cm high × 210 cm wide × 90 cm long, bunk bed, 147 cm high. There is distance of 67 cm between the two beds.■

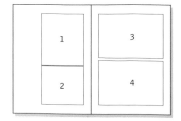

1. Study zone created with elements from the "Puzzle" system from Mixel▪

The wall panel enables the lamp, shelves and other accessories to be hooked directly onto the wall in such a way that they can be easily moved from one place to another and leads to the room being modified according to day to day necessities▪

2. Wall panel "Oh! Razio" from Zalf▪

This metal rail system can be equipped with different accessories which modify its function. Once a desk and various shelves have been added, it becomes a study zone▪

3. Composition from the program "Top Design" from Benicarló Moble 2000▪

The neutrality and simplicity of the wooden furniture transforms with the color of the accessories which allows the atmosphere of the room to be altered with a few simple changes▪

4. Bedroom composed of elements from the "Domino 3.1" system designed by Matteo Perego and Francesco Lucchese for Di Liddo & Perego▪

This group combines a finish in light ash with metal elements and lacquered surfaces. Both the bed and the computer table have castors so that the room can be rearranged according to necessities▪

The following pages:

Bedroom decorated with furniture from Galli▪

Oak with a natural finish has been combined with surfaces lacquered in white and violet. The opening mattress base of the bed "Donnie" allows for it to be used as a container. Half of the wardrobe is used as a study zone▪

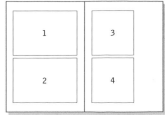

1	3
2	4

1 and 3. Convertible furniture group from Clei∎

This piece of furniture integrates a wardrobe that converts into a work zone and sofa supported by a fold-away panel which in turn hides a comfortable double bed. In this way, the space completely changes from day to night∎

2. Composition from the system "ON LINE" from Quelli della Mariani∎

This program offers the maximum in surface storage space. The bookcase is made up of open and closed elements which stamps dynamism on the study zone∎

4. Elements from the program "DOMINO 3.1". Designed by Francesco Lucchese and Matteo Perego for Di Liddo & Perego∎

The bed is situated under the bridging wardrobe that stands out for its original module with sliding doors in translucent glass that allow for the interior to be viewed slightly∎

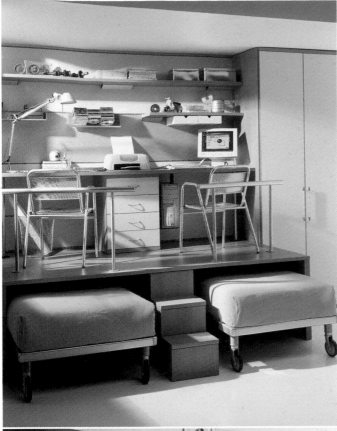

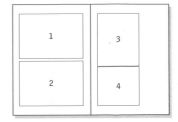

1	3
2	4

1 and 2. Transformable furniture designed by Clei∎
The impeccable design of this furniture allows the aspect that the room has during the day to be completely changed upon nightfall. The extensive area dedicated to studying or being with friends converts into a bedroom with two beds∎

3. Proposals from Quelli della Mariani∎
This system offers an original solution to saving space. A study zone for two people has been arranged over a wooden platform while the empty space is used to store the beds with castors during the day∎

4. Composition from the "DOMINO 3.1" system. Design from Matteo Perego and Francesco Lucchese for Di Liddo & Perego∎
The bed with castors has an innovative base made in beech stained in a dark color which extends to fulfill the function of bedside table∎

The following pages:
Composition integrated by various elements from the "PUZZLE" system from Mixel∎
The boiserie style wall panel incorporates a system which allows a great variety of accessories to be hooked on to it. All of the elements match one another forming a flexible and perfectly integrated composition∎

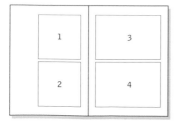

1 and 2. Transformable System "Nuo-voliolà" from Clei.

By day, this piece of furniture is a comfortable sofa. By night, with the help of no more than one movement, it becomes a double bed. The shelf rolls over and becomes the main support of the bed. Dimensions: 214.5 cm high × 172.9 cm wide × 104 cm (sofa position) / 208.3 cm long (bed position).

3. Modern bunk beds from the "Domino 3.1" program. Design from Matteo Perego and Francesco Lucchese for Di Liddo & Perego.

The upper bed slides along the wall panel while the lower one is on castors to facilitate movement.

4. Composition from the "Dedalo" program from IMA Mobili.

The elements in this room are arranged in an angle to make the most of the space. The rails on the wall panel allow for the easy movement of the sliding beds and study table.

The following pages:
Composition from the collection "City Line" from Doimo.

This bedroom is decorated with furniture of contemporary design in matching blue tones. The wardrobe with sliding doors combines surfaces in wood, plastic stained blue and aluminum trimmings.

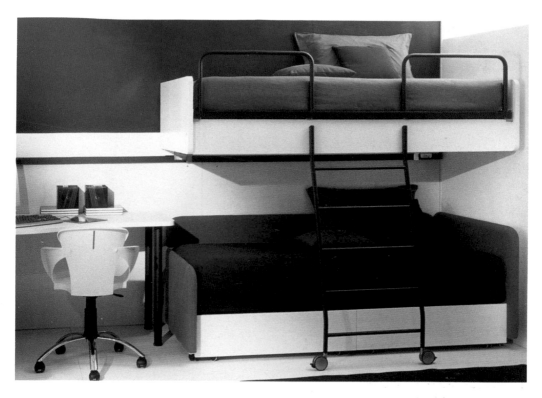

DIRECTORY

ASSOMOBILI
Via Manzoni, 54
22040 Alzate Brianza
(Como)
ITALY
Tel. 39 031 630 818
Fax 39 031 631 282
www.assomobili.com

AZCUE Y CIA S.A.
Olalde-Urrestilla, Apdo. 5
20730 Azpeitia
(Gipuzkoa)
SPAIN
Tel. 34 943 815 000
Fax 34 943 816 204
www.azcue.com

BABYMOBEL
Prolongación c/ de la
Albufera s/n
46430 Sollana (Valencia)
SPAIN
Tel. 34 961 740 616
Fax 34 961 740 642

BEBEFORM
Alan sok. Ugur
apt. Nº 9/1
81070 Saskinbakkal -
Estambul
TURKEY
Tel. 011 90 216 478 0255
Fax 011 90 216 359 0305
www.bebeform.com

Bébé-Jou
(IN SPAIN DISTRIBUTOR
PERELLÓ)
C/ Tánger, 53
08018 Barcelona
SPAIN
Tel. 34 933 091 516
Fax 34 933 097 282
www.bebe-jou.com

BELINO CREACIONES INFANTILES
POLÍGONO LA PEDRERA -
PARCELA 9, APDO. 11
46860 Albaida (Valencia)
SPAIN
Tel. 34 962 901 113
Fax 34 962 901 531
www.belino.es

BENICARLÓ MOBLE 2000
Ctra. N-340, Km 1045,200 -
Apdo. 82
12580 Benicarló (Castellón)
SPAIN
Tel. 34 964 467 320
Fax 34 964 467 321
www.bm2000.net

BOLIN BOLON (ARTEMUR)
Pol. Ind. La Polvorista;
C/ Ricote 2
30500 Molina from Segura
(Murcia)
SPAIN
Tel. 34 968 010 200

Fax 34 968 010 249
www.artemur.es

BOPITA
(LION INTERNATIONAL B.V.)
Edisonweg 3
6662 NW Elst (Gld)
THE NETHERLANDS
www.bopita.com

CARL HANSEN & SØN
Hansen Kochsgade 97 -
Postbox 225
DK 5100 Odense C.
DENMARK
Tel. 45 6612 1404
Fax 45 6591 6004
www.carlhansen.dk

CILEK MOBILYA A.S.
Kursunlu Sanayi Bölgesi
16420 Inegöl - Bursa
TURKEY
Tel. 90 224 721 2866
Fax 90 224 721 3070
www.cilek.com.tr

CLEI SRL
Via G. Marconi
22060 Carugo
(Como)
ITALY
Tel. 39 031 761666
Fax 39 031 762346
www.clei.it

CYRUS COMPANY
Via Mottarone 60
21010 Verghera di Samarate
(VA)
ITALY
Tel. 39 0331 224911
Fax 39 0331 721136
www.cyruscompany.it

CHICCO ESPAÑOLA S.A.
C/ Industrias, 10 - Pol.
Industrial Urtinsa, Apdo. 212
28923 Alcorcón (Madrid)
SPAIN
Tel. 34 916 499 000
Fax 34 916 413 224
www.chicco.es

DANONA, S. COOP.
Anardi Area 2 - Apdo. 42
20730 Azpeitia (Gipuzkoa)
SPAIN
Tel. 34 943 815 900
Fax 34 943 810 066
www.danona.com

DI LIDDO & PEREGO
Via Trieste 71
20036 Meda (MI)
ITALY
Tel. 39 0362 342290
Fax 39 0362 340320
www.diliddoeperego.it

DOIMO INTERNATIONAL GROUP
Via Montegrappa, 90
31010 Mosnigo di Moriago
(TV)
ITALY
Tel. 39 0438 890699

Fax 39 0438 890121
www.gruppodoimo.com

ERBA MOBILI
Via Don Guanella 28
22066 Mariano Comense
(CO)
ITALY
Tel. 39 031 746663
Fax 39 031 750624
www.erbamobili.it

FINN & HATTIE
(MAINE COTTAGE)
Post Office Box 539
04096 Yarmouth (Maine)
U.S.A.
Tel. 1 207 846 9166
Fax 1 207 846 9173
www.finnandhattie.com

FULI & C
C/ Barcelona s/n
08273 Santa Maria d'Oló
(BCN) - SPAIN
Tel. 34 938 385 003
Fax 34 938 384 014
fuli.co@terra.es

GALLI MOBILI
Via Alessandro Volta 3 - Loc.
Pilastrello
22060 Carugo (CO)
ITALY
Tel. 39 031 761368
Fax 39 031 762258
www.gallimobili.it

HEATHER SPENCER DESIGNS
Unit 22

Bradley Fold Trading Estate
Radcliffe Moor Road
BL2 6RT Bolton
Lancashire
UNITED KINGDOM
Tel. 44 01204 533224
Fax 44 01204 533992
www.hspencer.u-net.com

HÜLSTA WERKE GMBH
Gerhart-Hauptmann Str. 43-
49
D-48703 Stadtlohn
GERMANY
Tel. 49 0 2563/ 86-0
Fax 49 0 2563/ 86-1417
www.hueslta.de

I.M.A. MOBILI SPA
Via A. Manzoni, 27
33080 Prata di Pordenone
ITALY
Tel. 39 0434 612511
Fax 39 0434 621702
www.ima-mobili.it

JACADI
26 Rue Diderot
92028 Nanterre-Cedex
FRANCE
www.jacadi.fr

JULIA ARREDAMENTI
Via A. Carpené, 4
I-33070 Maron di Brugnera
(PN)
ITALY
Tel. 39 0434 616911
Fax 39 0434 6244453
www.julia-arreda.it

LEIPOLD
Alte Straße 1
D-96482 Ahorn
GERMANY
Tel. 49 0 9561/ 27000
Fax 49 0 9561/ 270027
www.leipold.de

LIVE AND PLAY
Postbus 43
3940 AA Doorn
THE NETHERLANDS
Tel. 0343 476276
Fax 0343 477708
www.liveandplay.nl

MARSHMALLOW COMPANY
170 West End Avenue, 12A
10023 New York, NY
U.S.A.
Tel. 1 212 799 0684
Fax 1 212 579 2234
www.marshmallowco.com

MICUNA
Prolongación c/ from la
Albufera s/n
46430 Sollana (Valencia)
SPAIN
Tel. 34 961 740 616
Fax 34 961 740 642
www.micuna.com

MIXEL (GRUPO TISETTANTA)
Via Tofane 37
20034 Giussano
ITALY
Tel. 39 0362 3191
Fax 39 0362 319300
www.tisettanta.com

MOBILIN
Passeig from Sant Joan, 165
08560 Manlleu (Barcelona)
SPAIN
Tel. 34 938 540 009
Fax 34 938 540 086
www.mobilin.com

PAIDI MÖBEL GMBH
Hauptstraße 87
D-97849 Hafenlohr
GERMANY
Tel. 49 0 93 91/501-0
Fax 49 0 93 94/501-160
www.paidi.de

PASITO A PASITO (TOYLAND,
S.A.)
Energía, 106 - Aptdo. 297
08940 Cornellá
(Barcelona)
SPAIN
Tel. 34 934 743 336
Fax 34 934 742 251
toyland@sefes.es

PERELLÓ
C/ Tánger, 53
08018 Barcelona
SPAIN
Tel. 34 933 091 516
Fax 34 933 097 282

QUELLI DELLA MARIANI
Via Toscani, 37
20038 Seregno (Mi)
ITALY
Tel. 39 0362 237020
Fax 39 0362 236915
www.quellidellamariani.it

SCHARDT GEORG KG
Am Riegel 15
D-96268 Mitwitz
GERMANY
Tel. 49 0 9266 9907 0
Fax 49 0 9266 9907 77
www.georg-schardt.de

SCHARDT
(IN SPAIN DISTRIBUTOR MN
PUERICULTURA 2000)
C/ Loreto, 17 H, entlo. 3
08029 Barcelona
SPAIN
Tel. 34 934 304 684
Fax 34 934 391 851

SOMETHING SPECIAL
240 Great Western Road
G4 9EJ Glasgow
Scotland
UNITED KINGDOM
Tel. 0141 332 5677
Fax 0141 3331215
www.somethingspecial.info

STOKKE
Av. from Vizcaya, 67
20800 Zarautz (Gipuzkoa)
SPAIN
Tel. 34 943 130 596
Fax 34 943 133 201
www.stokke.es

STOKKE FABRIKER AS
N-6260 Skodje
NORWAY
Tel. 47 702 44900
Fax 47 702 44990
www.stokke.com

TARANTINO STUDIO
1423 Main Street
08844 Millstone,
New Yersey
U.S.A.
Tel. 1 908 3592443
Fax 1 908 3590473
www.tarantinostudio.com

TARTINE ET CHOCOLAT
C/ Maestro Nicolau, 10
08021 Barcelona
SPAIN
Tel. 34 934 143 470
Fax 34 934 143 890
www.tartine-et-chocolat.com

TARTINE ET CHOCOLAT
Rue from Portalis 8 bis
75005 París
FRANCE
Tel. 33 1 58 221414
www.tartine-et-chocolat.com

THE CHILDREN'S FURNITURE
COMPANY
17 Trent Road

SW2 5BJ London
UNITED KINGDOM
Tel. 44 020 7737 7303
Fax 44 020 7326 4851
www.thechildrensfurniture
company.com

THE WHITE COMPANY
Unit 30
Perivale Industrial Park
Horsenden Lane South
UB6 7RJ Greenford
Middlesex
UNITED KINGDOM
Tel. 44 0870 900 9555
Fax 44 0870 900 9556
www.thewhiteco.com

TIEFFE MOBILI S.R.L.
Via S. Michele, 62
61020 Montecchio di
S. Angelo in Lizzola
(PU)
ITALY
Tel. 39 0721 498499
Fax 39 0721 499574
www.tieffemobili.it

Tirimilitin
C/ Laureà Miró 343-345
08950 Esplugues from Llo-
bregat
(Barcelona) - SPAIN
Tel. 34 933 711 802
Fax 34 933 711 810

WIGWAM KIDS
Unit 44
Bilston Glen Ind. Estate
Dryden Road
Loanhead
EH20 9NZ Edinburgh
Scotland
UNITED KINGDOM
Tel. 0870 902 7500
Fax 0131 448 0680
www.wigwamkids.co.uk

ZALF MOBILI COMPONIBILI SPA
Via Marosticana, 9
31010 Maser (TV)
ITALY
Tel. 39 04239255
Fax 39 0423 565866
www.gruppoeuromobil.com